Clutch Your Pearls, Girl!
Sister Wisdom to Protect Heart

By Stephanie L. McKenny

Clutch Your Pearls, Girl!
Sister Wisdom to Protect Your Heart

ISBN 10: 0-9705008-3-1
ISBN 13: 978-0-9705008-3-0
Copyright © 2010, J & J Publishing Company
A self-publishing company owned by
Stephanie L. McKenny

All rights reserved. No part of this book may be reproduced in any form, except for the inclusion of brief quotations in a review, without permission in writing from the author or publisher. Biblical quotes throughout this book come for the King James Version.

Clutch Your Pearls Dedication

*This book is dedicated to my daughter, **Crystal**. I also dedicate this book to all the women who have been abused in relationships and made it through and to all those women who are still struggling to break free.*

Contents

Precious Pearls Letter
Intro Part 1: The Proper Care & Handling of Pearls   8
Intro Part 2: The Attributes of Swine   11
Intro Part 3: Pearls and Swine Don't Mix   12

The Velvet Lined Box #1 – Perfecting Pearls for Purpose
Chapter 1: The Woman in the Mirror   17
Chapter 2: Wounds & Scars   27
Chapter 3: You Have Destiny   41

The Velvet Lined Box #2 – Displaced Pearls
Chapter 4: Giving Away Pearls   50
Chapter 5: Throwing Pearls   57
Chapter 6: Single Women & Married Men   61
Chapter 7: Make Him Love You?   65
Chapter 8: Why Does She Stay?   73

The Velvet Lined Box #3 – The Pearl Snatcher
Chapter 9: Leanness to Your Soul   80
Chapter 10: Outshining Him   91
Chapter 11: His Words   97
Chapter 12: Pearls in Isolation   103
Chapter 13: Stolen Pearls   108
Chapter 14: Him and Your Children   115
Chapter 15: Pray for Him   122

The Velvet Lined Box #4 – Pearls in Waiting
Chapter 16: Pearls in Waiting   127
Chapter 17: Marriage   132
Chapter 18: Recognizing a Good Man   139

Dear Precious Pearls,

    I call you precious pearls because you are a worthy treasure that should always be loved, valued and respected. You were fearfully and wonderfully made by the perfected hands of God. When God created you, He considered you to be one of His many masterpieces. Never in a million years did God desire for you to be mistreated in any of the relationships that you've encountered throughout your life. There was a reason why He calls you, BELOVED because that's what He wanted; for you to BE LOVED.

    I wrote this book with you in mind and for the many other precious pearls to come. I wanted you to be aware of how important it is to love yourself while loving your God. I felt compelled to tell you this because I didn't want you to compromise, submit or succumb to mistreatment in your relationships with men. It's a fact; men will treat you according to how you allow them to. They recognize their boundaries the minute they've been in your company. And even though they may try to cross them, they really can't unless you give them permission to do so.

Please understand, I didn't write this book to discredit men at all. There are so many good men all over this world. They were created in the image of God just like you. I must pause for a moment to applaud all the good men for all they do to enforce healthy loving relationships (Kudos to good men!).

My focus, my mission and my call is to make you aware of the signs and characteristics of those men who choose to mistreat women along with helping you to recognize how valuable you really are.

Sister, it's time to **Clutch Your Pearls, Girl!** Grab a hold of your integrity, your self-esteem; hang onto your dreams and your virginity (or your commitment to be celibate). Grasp your self-respect, your ambition and do everything you can to protect your heart with all diligence because if you don't someone will come along and try desperately to snatch your pearls.

It is my prayer that you will take this journey throughout these pages and glean from the sisterly wisdom shared from my heart to yours. -----

Lovingly written, Stephanie L. McKenny

Clutch Your Pearls

"Give not that which is holy unto the dogs, neither cast ye your pearls before swine, lest they trample them under their feet, and turn again and rend you."

Introduction 1:
The Proper Care & Handling of Pearls

When you think of pearls, you think of a piece of jewelry that is elegant, sophisticated and classy. Pearls are not meant to be worn everyday, but when they are worn they capture the eyes of those that behold them. Pearls are considered very valuable in the eyes of its owner. Usually they are placed in a special velvet-lined box; not mixed with other jewelry. They are sacred and used only for special occasions. The pearls are never given out; unless there is, an intimate relationship already established such as the one that exists between a mother and daughter. They are never mishandled or thrown away. They are treasured.

Pearls take up to 3-5 years to develop so when they are found, they are considered to be of great worth. Because of their rarity and value, not everyone knows how to properly care and handle them. The fragile coat of precious pearls makes them prone to scratches and scarring from everyday activities. An owner of pearls must consider the following in order to safeguard them from abuse:

- VALUE YOUR PEARLS. An owner of pearls must value them so every effort is made to protect them from being damaged. When we value our pearls we are less prone to let any and everyone handle them without proving their worthiness. Women must carry this same kind of high degree of value for themselves. Doing so, will protect them from being mishandled and improperly cared for.
- SEPARATE YOUR PEARLS. Pearls should never be mixed with other jewelry in a jewelry box. Pearls should be stored separately and you must lay them flat, lengthwise. Costume Jewelry and Pearls have no correlation. Held up against one another, there is a distinct difference. As women, we can't hang around or entertain everyone's company. Some people are not meant to be in our lives and we must be willing to draw the separating line that keeps the good from the bad.
- GUARD YOUR PEARLS. You must be mindful of what you expose your pearls to. You shouldn't expose them to your perfume, hair products or makeup, because those chemicals can cause

damage. As women, we must guard our heart with diligence so we don't allow ourselves to open a door that could be damaging to our spirit, our integrity, our purpose and our ability to love and be loved.

- AND never, never, never cast your pearls before swine.

Introduction 2: The Attributes of Swine

Swine as we know them are unclean animals that are accustomed to mingling with other swine, getting dirty and eating slop. Swine have no intentions of getting clean and everyone they come in contact with has the potential of being covered with mud or slop. The mindset of swine simply regards the pig pen as heaven on earth. Anyone who enters into his world is bound to feel the blunt of his snorts (the negative words), his smell (his negative character) and his slop (his negative treatment). In their eyes, anything thrown to them while there in the pig pen is considered something for them to eat or to trample on. Even if something as elegant and as classy as a pearl is thrown their way, it is inevitable that the swine will trample on it and rend it to pieces. Their mindset does not even consider the elegance of a pearl. They feel sloppy, look sloppy and do whatever they can to make others get sloppy along with them. If you're not careful they will swallow and consume your precious pearls whole.

"Give not that which is holy unto the dogs, neither cast ye your pearls before swine, lest they trample them under their feet, and turn again and rend you."
~ Matthew 7:6, KJV

"For truth is precious and divine, too rich a pearl for carnal swine."
~ Samuel Butler, English novelist

Introduction 3:
Pearls & Swine Don't Mix

As I was reading the Bible one day, the scripture mentioned above caught my eye, or should I say caught the attention of my spirit. Matthew 7 is a passage of scripture that I have read many times throughout the years of my salvation walk, but on this particular day, the text jumped right at me. As I meditated on the scripture, my past relationships and many of the relationships I'd watched other women engage in began to dance through my mind.

It later dawned on me that there are many women all over the world involved in, stuck in or about to encounter unhealthy, toxic relationships. I also realized that it didn't matter what kind of woman it was; women each and everyday were settling for unhealthy relationships and casting their precious pearls before swine.

In this book, pearls are symbolic to the many beautiful women that God has fearfully and wonderfully made in His likeness and image. These pearls are the women who are precious, valuable and have a divine purpose for their existence. They are the women who survive the toughest storms without bitterness residing in their hearts. When odds are against them there is a fight within that causes them to rise and press forward. They are the women who strive to love and nurture those who come in their midst. They are influential; they are survivors. They are phenomenal. Our pearls are a representation of our heart and body; parts of us that should be handled delicately, shared cautiously and considered valuable in our own eyes.

Pearls also represent the gifts and talents we possess as women. God has equipped us with so much potential. We have the ability to accomplish our greatest goal because that enablement resides within. With God on our side, nothing can defeat us unless we yield to defeat's cry. It is vital to remember, however, that no matter how great the challenge, defeat was never our destiny. Victory has always been the desired outcome for our lives. So my question is this: Why are so many women dealing with a cycle of defeat?

Perhaps, the reason has to do with the care and handling of our pearls. Where have we been casting them? Who have we been giving them to? Giving away our pearls is symbolic to giving away our heart and not everybody should have access to our heart.

Swine, for the purposes of this book, are symbolic to the many men who have degraded, mistreated and abused women all over the world. They are the men who have believed the value of a woman has depreciated. Many of them have failed to realize that women are a part of God's creation and were made from man and for man. We were created for the purpose of helping man and because God thought it was not good for man to be alone.

Never was a woman meant to be mistreated, disrespected, manipulated, or abused by man. He was to love her, and she was to submit to him. Adam began this cycle of love in the garden when he addressed Eve after God presented her to him. He said, "Woman, bone of my bone and flesh of my flesh (Genesis 2)." She was a part of him and he was a part of her. Notice that Adam didn't say, "break her bone or beat her flesh." This kind of treatment was unheard of in the first marriage and should not be a part of your life either.

By no means am I demeaning men and their profound role of responsibility. Men are a part of God's creation and everything that God made was good. There are many men throughout the world who are great leaders, entrepreneurs, doctors, lawyers, counselors, pastors, coaches, mentors, husbands, and fathers. There are good men all over this world. Not every man is a cheater, gay or in jail. Not every man treats a woman the way swine treat pearls as stated in the scripture. There are some men who are likened unto kings who are searching for their queens. There are some men who are ready to love, to commit and to be faithful to one woman. Will that woman be you?

Knowing the vast differences between pearls and swine, I've come to the conclusion that pearls and swine don't mix. This kind of connection, a swinish relationship, could be a horrendous experience to the woman who gets entangled in it. Don't get me wrong, the love connection between a man and a woman can be beautiful. It is my prayer that you experience love— God's way. It is my goal to help you recognize that pearls and swine don't mix. They never did and they never will.

The Velvet Lined Box #1
Perfecting Pearls for Purpose

Chapter 1: The Woman in the Mirror

"Mirror, mirror on the wall, who's the fairest of them all?" This is the question the wicked queen in the children's story, *Snow White*, constantly asked while looking in the mirror. Her intent was to seek affirmation of her worth and beauty.

Many of us today are just like that queen because we look for someone to validate us. Inwardly, every woman longs to hear someone tell them she is beautiful. Yes, we want to hear that we are the fairest of them all.

Even though this kind of affirmation is welcomed by most women, we must not allow ourselves to become dependent upon receiving compliments from those who behold our beauty. Dependency upon those declarations of our beauty and worth from others may cause our opinion of who we are to be contingent upon their point of view only.

This is exactly what happened to the wicked queen in *Snow White*. She limited herself to the opinion of the masked face in the mirror to determine her beauty. For some odd reason, she needed this validation. Because of the position she held as queen, she should have known she was beautiful and a woman of great worth.

Being created in the image of God so long ago gave us all the validation we needed to recognize our worth. God's opinion of who we are far exceeds the opinion of others; however, there are some women who allow themselves to feed off the approval and opinions of others to make them feel good. Whether we realized it or not, many of us have been seeking the approval of others since we were little girls.

You remember when you did your first cartwheel, said your first speech or had a part in your first school play. You looked to your parents and/or guardians to see their reaction. You wanted to make sure that what you did met their approval. The minute you didn't receive approval from others you began thinking that you weren't good enough. This same attitude has followed many of us into our adulthood and within our relationships. If we're not careful, it can cause us to become dependent upon the approval of others to sustain our peace of mind. When involved with a swinish man this can become very disappointing because he never approves of anything you do. In his eyes, you can't do anything right.

Here's a little sister wisdom for you: who cares what he or anyone else thinks of you! It doesn't matter how others see or think of you; what matters the most is how you see and think of yourself. Beauty is in the eyes of the beholder. Wipe your eyes or clean your eyeglasses and begin to see yourself the way God sees you; one of the best parts of His creation. You were fearfully and wonderfully made. There is only one you, and that should be enough validation to confirm your significance in the eyes of God.

From the beginning, the image of mankind was destined to be perfect because we were created in the image of God (Genesis 1:26-27). Obviously our image was important because we are the only part of creation that was created in God's likeness and image. Yes, we initially had it going on! The Word of God is a reflection of who we are to become. From the beginning, God anticipated for us to walk in the fullness of that image and to exercise the authority freely given to us. As we progressed through life, however, our overall experiences and the words expressed to and about us caused many of us to detour from following the image of God. We ended up in places we wished we would've never gone and done some things we wished we would've never done. We found ourselves right back in front of that same magical mirror the wicked queen viewed in *Snow White*, seeking for someone to tell us how good and beautiful we are. If we took the time to look at ourselves through the image of God (His Word), no one would be able to tell us we weren't good enough, much less that we weren't the fairest of them all, because we would know it for ourselves.

This whole idea of knowing it for yourself goes back to how you see yourself. How you see yourself affects your life in many facets. It will affect your appearance and your conduct, and it will also affect the kinds of relationships that you will get involved with.

If you don't feel worthy enough to be treated well in a relationship, you will find yourself quickly connecting to men who will treat you any kind of way. If you don't have any expectations or set standards within your relationships, then the men you involve with will treat you how they think you ought to be treated. And sometimes that is not what you were looking for. Have expectations and set standards that you are willing to live by so others will honor your stance.

If you don't recognize that you are a pearl, you'll find yourself casting your heart before a swinish man, and the rending will begin. He will stalk you like a pig pursuing its slop. He is prepared to do whatever it takes to ultimately belittle you, talk you out of your dreams and block you from recognizing who you really are in God. I can confidently say the results of a swinish relationship never end very well. Pearls have no business entertaining company with swine.

His kind of company or the relationship he is so desperately trying to entangle you in is not worth forfeiting everything you've achieved. You're too precious and have too much to offer to allow anyone to treat you inappropriately. Whether you realize it or not, you deserve to be treated right, you deserve to be loved and you deserve to be in a healthy, loving relationship.

Sometimes a woman who has been involved with swinish men in previous relationships and who also suffers from low self-esteem may feel she will never experience a healthy and loving relationship. She may deeply desire to have a good man in her life and want to be treated right; but strangely as it seems, even when a good man comes into her life she will either drain him or she will feel like she is not worthy to be involved with him.

When you struggle with low self-image, it will cause you to drain the man in your life because you will always look to him to make you feel good about yourself or you will always wonder if you're good enough. Doing so will let you down every time. A man is not going to compliment you every single day, ten times a day, just to make you feel good. Not only will he feel drained, but he will also feel pressured to build you up. When he doesn't fulfill that requirement, it will only create friction in the relationship. He will eventually grow tired of it and will move on. A woman should have at least some degree of self-confidence about her. Men look for women that can hold their own if need be.

When a good man enters the life of a woman who has low self-esteem, at times she may begin to think that the good man is too good to be true and in her mind she thinks there has to be something wrong with him. Even though he treats her with respect, treats her children well and doesn't make any sexual advances, she automatically thinks something has got to be wrong with this man. In actuality, he is a good man and because some women don't know how a good man is supposed to treat them, they kick him to the curb with no explanation. Some women may even say, "He's too nice." As if being nice makes a man weak. In his ability to be nice, he's actually showing you how good he will treat you. Needless to say, when you don't feel good about you and you've previously been involved in swinish relationships that belittled you, it becomes difficult to see the good in a good man.

I remember being just like that. I met someone who was a complete gentleman that treated me with great respect. He accepted me for who I was and he even took great interest in my daughter's well-being; yet, I couldn't see it. I thought it was too good to be true. My self-esteem was so low at the time that I didn't think I was good enough for him. He was well-educated, financially stable, a minister of the Gospel, owned a house, and was successful in his career. I thought he couldn't possibly want someone who wasn't as educated as him and someone who had a child out of wedlock. He couldn't possibly want a ready-made family, I thought. In my eyes, I was a grasshopper, and he was one of the giants in the land. At that time, I let a good man out of my life.

This is why it is so important that, before beginning any relationship, you need to feel good about you. You can't properly love anyone unless you first love yourself. Scripture clearly tells us that we must love our neighbor as we love ourselves (Matthew 22:39), but many of us fail in this because we've forgotten to love ourselves.

I challenge you to begin loving who you are right now. You may not be perfect, but loving who you are now will help you to grow and develop into all that you desire to become.

It is a process that begins with changing the way you think about yourself. Just because others have said negative things about you for so long, doesn't mean you have to live out those words. You must eradicate those words from your mind. What you deserve is not contingent upon what others think, but it falls back on what you think and how you feel about yourself. Begin to think highly of yourself. Believe me, doing so is not going to hurt you, but it will help you to recognize how blessed you really are.

Thinking highly of yourself does not mean you are conceited or uppity. There are some men that have a problem with women who think they are the fairest of them all. When you walk around with confidence and embrace independence, it becomes threatening to swinish men. This is only because they now feel inferior to you and your presence is intimidating.

Keep in mind, that a swinish man wants to be in control and when he feels he's lost the upper hand, he will begin to make you feel bad about feeling good about yourself. He starts off by criticizing your abilities, your appearance or your friends and associates. He will even tell you, "You think you're better than everybody." "You think you're so perfect." These words are only spoken with the intent to discourage you.

He will attack anything that makes you happy. His purpose for doing so is to make you feel like a small fearful child who has disobeyed her parents and runs in a corner awaiting punishment. In that corner you will remain if you continue to allow him to put you there.

Just because he may suffer from his own insecurities and low self-esteem, don't allow his inadequacies to affect who you are and how you feel about yourself. Don't allow his issue to become your issue.

Raise your level of thinking and your love for yourself. Reflect on the image of God by looking at the greatest mirror you could ever stand before—the Word of God—and know that you are worthy of the best. God fixed it that way a long time ago.

Take a moment to look at the woman in the mirror. Look into your eyes. Your eyes tell your story. What do you see? Do you see yourself as being the fairest of them all? How do you feel about yourself? Do you see that you deserve to be treated with respect? Do you see that you deserve to be loved? Being honest to these few simple questions will reveal whether or not you possess a healthy self-image.

If you recognize that you are suffering from a low self-image, there are ways you can rebuild it pearl by pearl. Listed below are a few pearls of wisdom to consider for remodeling your self image.

Pearls of Wisdom

- Connecting to God through His Word will reveal your value. Feast on these words, believe them and walk in them.
- Change your thinking about yourself (Proverbs 23:7). It really doesn't matter what others think of you, but what really matters is what you think of yourself.
- Speak positively over your life (Proverb 18:21) daily.
- Love yourself first so you can love others effectively.

Chapter 2: Wounds & Scars

Remember when you were a little girl and you fell down for the first time? You cried and then ran to your mother in hopes that she would make you feel better. She would grab you, give you a hug to calm you down and then begin working on your bruise. She would clean it, put some first-aid ointment on it and cover it with a bandage. From that point on, the healing process began.

As you can see, covering the wound with a bandage is the initial remedy. The number of days the wound should be covered is determined by the severity of the wound itself. Initially, the bandages are applied so the wound won't be hit again, which could create a more serious injury or additional pain. No one wants to be hit again especially if the wound hasn't completely healed; yet, the bandages were not meant to remain on the wound forever.

The analogy mentioned above is what takes place when we are wounded physically; however, the wounds I am referring to are the disappointments you've encountered, the negative words spoken in your ears that still linger in your spirit, the emotional scars from life experiences and possibly the physical scars from abusive relationships.

Many of us have handled our hurting experiences by covering them up, hoping that in time we would heal; needless to say, some of us continued to be hit over and over again with the same kind of hurt. In response to never wanting to hurt again, we built a wall around us, put our masks on and swept it all under the rug without totally healing from the emotional scars that were left behind. Healing was in view, but forgiving was totally out of the question.

When we have experienced being hurt by someone we love, we find it at times difficult to heal; much less forgive. The length of time for the healing process is determined by the severity of the hurt, the individual that hurt you and how long the hurtful experience took place. Sometimes we think we've been healed, but in actuality we've allowed ourselves to suppress it in our subconscious. We actually made it go away in our mind. Of course we later realized, when we've been "hit again" with the same kind of hurt or hurt by the same person that the wound was never really completely healed in the first place. We just packed it down and covered it up.

It's similar to when someone brings up an old incident (an old boyfriend, a childhood experience or a bad separation or divorce). You are quick to say; "I'm fine. I don't even think about it anymore." And, as those words are leaving your mouth, your insides are still cringing with the feelings of that old hurt. You realize then that you really haven't quite gotten over what they did to you. If you can't talk about it or deal with others discussing it, then it's possible you still need to be healed from it.

I can remember a tough time in my life when I was deeply hurt by someone I loved. They hurt me continually on and off for years, but I packed it down and kept it covered and tried to convince myself daily that it really didn't bother me anymore. As far as I was concerned, I was over it.

In the beginning, when the hurt first occurred, moving towards forgiveness was a struggle for me because I felt justified for not letting it all go. I held it for years, kept it covered so no one could see my hurt or the bitterness that had begun to set in my heart. Soon I noticed that my love for this person began to change; it grew cold. Nevertheless, I continued to go to church and continued to follow my daily routines. As the Word of

God kept coming forth from the pulpit concerning forgiveness, the wall I had built so perfectly around me began to crumble down. After hearing the Word, I felt exposed before the Lord. I realized then that I had to forgive. Only at that point, could God mend my heart and take me through the healing process. Through being honest with God about how I felt concerning this situation, hearing His Word and applying what I heard in my life, I got through and I was able to forgive and love that person again.

Part of your healing will begin when you are totally honest with yourself and with God. You have to confront those emotional wounds and allow God to uproot all that stuff that was never planted by Him in the first place. Not dealing with it will never heal it. Healing is a process. Some wounds have a way of healing on their own; while others take more time and require more of our effort. No matter how much time is required for you to heal emotionally, go after your healing because being healed is far better than being broken. Being broken is not a place in which you want to remain. You were meant to be healed. God designed your body that way.

Initially, the covering of the wound is important to the healing process. The formation of the scab is just as important. There are several purposes for the scab. The presence of the scab is part of the healing process as well. Actually, this is one of the signs that your body is healing itself. It is so amazing how God actually formed our physical body to heal itself (Kudos for God!). The scab is a protective cap over the wound that helps to prevent dirt and germs from entering the wound. It also helps to limit your level of blood loss, guard the wound against infection and stabilizes the wound. Plus, while the scab is forming, underneath the scab new skins cells are being formed. The scab remains firmly in place until this process is complete.

I liken the scab that forms on the wound to God's way of covering and comforting us in the midst of the tough times in our lives. In the midst of our hurtful experiences, God will give us just what we need to comfort, protect and strengthen us again. Underneath the disappointments, hurt and abuse is a pearl waiting to be resurfaced. Yes, you are coming out of that rubble! Allow God to heal you from the inside out so you can become a better you.

Becoming better and experiencing the best in our relationships is something we all want to attain, but there are times when we find ourselves on a continual cycle of being hurt. After you've been hurt several times in different relationships, you might begin to ask, "Why is this happening to me?" or "Why does this keep happening to me?" For some reason you keep meeting the same kind of men who keep hurting you. Has your self-esteem level dropped so low that you've settled for mistreatment in a relationship? Have you begun to recognize that you are beginning to compromise your standards just to be in the arms of a man? Questions like these will help you to determine whether these kinds of hurtful relationships are happening because of you, him or both of you.

Unfortunately, some of the wounds we suffered from were created by us. I know you're saying, "You've got to be kidding me? Why would I bring this on myself?" Hear me out. No one really likes to admit that they are the reason for their hurt, but in some cases we really are to blame. This is because many of us have allowed individuals in our lives that didn't know how to handle our heart. We allowed these people to mistreat us even though we knew deep within ourselves that we deserved better. The red flag, the stop sign and all the warning signals were all there in the beginning to prompt us to walk away from the very relationship that in the end seemed to hurt us the most. We gave them an inch and they took the whole field! Sometimes we tolerated the mistreatment just so we would have someone in our lives. Open your eyes and stop falling for that foolishness. The package may look good to the eyes, but the contents are definitely unacceptable.

Then again, it might be him. Sometimes the wounds are formed because someone else is to blame. You did everything right, the connection was there and the relationship seemed to be going so well and then it happens. He drops you—with no explanation and no warning as if you were just another woman to add to his player list. Out of the blue he starts putting you down, humiliating you in public and then he hits you that very first time. What you are experiencing is the real 'him' beginning to surface beyond his display of kind character. I'm sure he kept his swinish ways hidden for as long as he could. It was inevitable that in a matter of time he would take off his sheep clothing and expose his swinish character (Remember we're talking about swinish men only because a good man will always know how to love and respect a lady).

Unfortunately when you get involved with a swinish man he usually doesn't care about you or anything that has to do with you. He really doesn't understand how to care for, much less how to treat a woman. He likes to play mind games and he will belittle anything about you. He wants control. In his eyes he thinks he's Mr. Right, but little does he know his stuff is stinking louder than a pile of pig's slop. He's in the pig pen snorting at your very presence hoping you'll be fool enough to come in to eat his slop. Abusive men and men with unhealthy characteristics need help, and, usually, the people they get involved with aren't the ones who help them. Stay away from swinish men (abusers: physical, verbal, spiritual, sexual and emotional) because the end results of these kinds of relationships could cost you your life—literally.

Sometimes both of you need inner healing. When two wounded people get involved in a relationship together, one of two things will happen; either the two of you will continue to hurt each other, or someone will get enough courage to leave the relationship. Leaving the relationship is what you need to strongly consider. Holding onto someone who continually hurts you is foolish. You should love yourself better than that. Believe me; you won't be lonely without him. Rather, you'll be at peace. Walk away and take time to heal.

When we don't take the time to heal from our hurt, usually the hurt begins to grow and take other forms. It will affect any relationship you are connected to. Before you know it, you're going off on people at the drop of a hat. This is because hurt people hurt other people. When you are filled with frustration and bitterness, you're not easy to forgive and have not healed from the hurts in your past; you will hurt others until you completely heal. We see this cycle occurring when abused people abuse others. Even though the abused person hated the abuse while it was happening to them, ironically the abused later becomes the abuser.

If you don't take the time to heal, you will find yourself trying to fill a void in your life with any man who comes along. I don't know how it's possible, but somehow our hurt attracts others who hurt. If a woman comes out of an abusive relationship, she must be very careful when she gets involved in her next relationship. She must make sure she takes the time to heal; otherwise, she may find herself in the same kind of relationship. At first she may not notice it, but as she continues in the relationship she may later realize that the same characteristics of the person who hurt her in the first place are now in the new person she's currently involved herself with.

The hurt, if not dealt with, will follow you into the next relationship whether you intended it to or not. Some people call it, "old baggage." You can't bring it into a relationship and expect the relationship to last. When we carry "old baggage" into a new relationship, the new man involved with you tends to suffer because of the emotional damage that the former companion inflicted on you. If he's a good man, that's not fair to him because he didn't hurt you; he only wants to love you. It's good to have your guard up, but don't make him suffer for what someone else did to you.

The Bible shares with us how new wine shouldn't be poured into old skins (Matthew 9:17) because the bottles will break. You can't expect to be treated as delicately as a pearl by jumping from one relationship to the next without first being healed. A new relationship never heals the old wounds. It's a temporary fix. Ask the woman at the well (John 4). I'm sure she can give you an earful about jumping in and out of relationships and how her thirst was never quenched. (It wasn't until she met the best man ever…His name was Jesus!) Getting a new man in your life is not what healing is all about. He really isn't your source of healing; he's just another form of cover-up.

Covering up your hurt never completes the healing; it only soothes you temporarily. Have you ever had one of those closets or one of those rooms that no one is allowed to go in? It's a room or closet filled with so much junk that if anyone tried to come in they would be bombarded with clothing, old books, old pictures, old toys, and a whole bunch of other stuff nobody uses anymore or refuses to throw away. Yet, all that stuff stays in there until someone has the courage to clean it up. This is how we do when we've been wounded. We throw it all in a room; shut the door and walk away thinking the stuff is going to go away. Many of us believe that if we don't deal with it, it will go away. This is not always the case when it comes to becoming emotionally healed. Sooner or later we will have to address it. Not dealing with it doesn't make it go away; nor does it heal us. Many of us have done such a good job with packing it down, sweeping it under the rug and putting on our mask to display our strength, but inwardly we are suffering in silence. I call it the cover-up phases in our lives.

The cover-up phase comes in different forms. Some women have resorted to drugs, alcohol, sex, and working extensively to ease the pain of their hurt. They use things and people to camouflage the hurt they've managed to keep packed down for a long time. Women who use these methods will never experience true healing.

Some women resort to connecting with God as a means to heal their wounds. Of course, running to God for comfort is ideal, scriptural and highly recommended. Yet, there are many women in church who are hurting and are still trying to portray that they have everything together. They are more concerned about what other people will say or how other people will perceive them as a Christian woman. They will jump around the church and shout when the praises go up, they will speak in other tongues, shake and even quote scriptures verbatim and still be hurting. I'm not downing the church or God. I'm writing this because I know. I've been there. Yes, you can be saved, sanctified and filled with the Holy Ghost but still hurt. Suffering in silence because you don't want anyone to know what you're dealing with because it might portray to others that you are a weak Christian.

Sister, it's time to take the mask off and allow God to begin the healing process in your heart. The enemy wants you to suffer in silence. He wants you to keep that hurt and bitterness in your heart so you won't ever love or be loved again, but the devil is a liar! The Church is a place of healing. Change takes place when we enter into the house of worship and hear God's Word. If you have to cry out in the service, roll on the floor, run to the altar for prayer; do it. Don't worry about what others will think or what they will say. You need to be whole. Focus on that.

There are times even after we've experienced wholeness when the scars are still there. Even though the scars from the old hurt may still be there, you don't need to continue to be hurt by it. Have you ever looked at your body and noticed the scars still on your body? Its funny how some scars heal totally, some fade away and others still remain on our bodies. Scars are reminders of what happened and of what God brought us through. Even though the scar is still there, you know that you've been healed.

Knowing that you've been healed is your breakthrough moment. Yes, the scar is there and yes, the situation did happen in your life, but it doesn't have to hurt anymore. That's exactly where God wants you to be…where it doesn't hurt anymore. Reach out to God and allow Him to get you to that point. Let Him put you on the potter's wheel and make you over again (Jeremiah

18). Momma did a good job in comforting you when you fell down, but God knows exactly how to comfort you far beyond momma's touch.

Pearls of Wisdom

- Forgive yourself. Refuse to remember what God has chosen to forget.
- Forgive those that hurt you. Relinquish your right to punish those who hurt you by hanging on to their transgression. Allow the Lord to deal with them.
- Covering up old hurt never completes the healing; it only soothes you temporarily. Allow God to heal the areas in your life that you are so desperately trying to hide.
- All God to heal you because being healed is far better than being broken.

Chapter 3: You Have Destiny

You have destiny! Your future looks far brighter than your past. Regardless of what may have happened to you yesterday, last week, last year, or even in your childhood; your future looks far greater than your past. There is something unique about you. It's true. When God created you He broke the mold. Your fingerprint is completely different from any other person's in the world—that is phenomenal. Not only are you unique, but your very presence was so significant to God that He created a divine plan for your existence (Jeremiah 29:11). Yes, you have destiny and you are here on purpose! No matter how you got here (two-parent family, single-parent family or adoption) you are not an accident; your life is purposeful. You were created to succeed and not to fail.

God never wanted you to forfeit the gifts, talents and dreams He has strategically placed in you. He has given you everything you need to survive and make it in this life (II Peter 1:3). God made an investment in your life a long time ago. When God made this investment, His intentions were for you to utilize all that He gave you. Those dreams were never meant to follow you in the grave unfulfilled; rather, they were meant to be exposed for the world to see.

If you stay yielded to God's direction, He will establish a platform for your gifts and talents to be displayed before many. Yes, your gifts will make room for you and bring you before great men (Proverbs 18:16). Like I said, your future looks greater than your past. There is something you have to accomplish that is beyond your imagination. Believe in you, believe in your dreams and pursue your destiny. Don't allow anyone to stop you from believing in your dreams. Be careful of the dream killers. Don't allow anyone to talk you out of your destiny and your purpose for living.

Who you connect with does affect the level of persistency you take to reach your goals. Don't allow yourself to get in a relationship with a man who does not believe in you or where you're going in life. If he doesn't believe in your dreams (vision) and where you're going in life (destiny), he will become a hindrance to it. This may be done intentionally or unintentionally, but it will be done. If he happens to be a swinish man, he doesn't believe in you anyway. He doesn't see your destiny the way you do. It doesn't interest him. In essence, he doesn't think it's going to happen for you. The only thing a swinish man wants you to do is focus on him and his goals, if he has any. If he's doing nothing, he doesn't want you to do anything.

A good man doesn't carry himself that way. When a good man comes into your life, he will motivate you to go after your dreams. He will make every effort to help you achieve. He won't be jealous, and he definitely won't talk you out of what rightfully belongs to you.

God definitely doesn't want anyone to come into your life who will talk you out of going after your goals, vision and dreams. I am reminded of the story of Jacob and Esau (Genesis 25:29-34) where Esau gave up his birthright for food. Esau had been working in the field and he was hungry to the point of feeling faint. Esau allowed his brother to swindle him out of a blessing—out of his destiny. Jacob talked Esau right out of his birthright. Jacob preyed on Esau's vulnerability at the time. At Esau's weakest point, Jacob seized the opportunity to get what he wanted. There are a few lessons to glean from this biblical story.

Lesson one: A woman shouldn't allow a man to see her as being weak. Yes, we are considered the weaker vessel, but by no means are we weak. As we draw from God's strength, we will become as strong as we need to be. When we become too dependent upon a man, or anyone for that matter; it gives them too much power over our lives. Before you know it, they'll run your life. Showing yourself as being overly dependent gives men the impression that you are needy and weak. As a result, they will walk all over you.

Lesson two: Don't allow someone to sabotage what you worked so hard to achieve. People who try to sabotage your success are like party poopers. They are the people who try their hardest to spoil your success story. When you begin to recognize that the man in your life wants you to give up on your dreams and goals, a red flag should go up immediately in your mind. He won't tell you directly to your face that he wants you to give up your dreams. He will subtly convince you to redirect your energy somewhere else. Watch out! He's a dream killer.

He knows you have gifts, talent and a vision for your life. However, because he's not at center stage, he'll try his best to sabotage it or either attempt to talk you out of it. One other thing, because he knows you're gifted, he may also be intimidated by your future success. He doesn't want you to move ahead of him. He knows you have what it takes, but because he's not going anywhere, he doesn't want you to either.

The objective of a swinish man is to make every attempt possible to belittle you so bad with the intentions of killing your confidence so that you won't even attempt to move forward towards your divine purpose in life. The swinish man hates to see you succeed and finds it humorous when you fail. Before you know it, he's convinced you that you can't do what God is prompting in your spirit to fulfill. Slowly you'll stop dreaming, and your goals and aspirations will seem far fetched.

The zeal, the tenacity will fade away slowly as if it never existed. I beseech you my dear sister, you woman of great vision; stop listening to that garbage. That's enough of the lies. Shake yourself! Ask God to show you the vision again. You have to start believing and dreaming again. God has placed too much in you for you to turn back on it now.

Lesson three: Don't let a man or anyone else talk you out of your dreams, goals and/or vision for your life. Don't give a man so much power in your life where you begin to value his words so much that he has the ability to talk you out of pursuing your dreams. For that matter, don't let him talk you out of your joy, peace of mind, salvation, or remaining abstinent until you are married. His words and influence should never have that much power.

Being talked out of what rightfully belongs to you is something that occurred many years ago before we were even created. It all began in the Garden of Eden when the serpent beguiled Eve (Genesis 3:1-6). Initially, the serpent posed a trick question, *"Yea, hath God said, ye shall not eat of every tree of the garden?"* The serpent posed this question to see where Eve stood. Symbolically, swinish men want to find out if you know who you are and what you stand for. They want to see if you have set boundaries, and if so, if you're willing to step beyond them. What he's doing is making an assessment about your actions to determine whether you would compromise your integrity, your salvation, your dreams, your body or even your very life. Swinish men want to know how easy or how hard it will be to get you to eat his slop without a fight. Our adversary also wants to know how easy or hard it will be to get you to feast on his lies.

Eve confidently tells the serpent what she can and cannot do (Genesis 3:2-3). She makes her boundaries clear to the serpent. It's similar to when you went out on a date with someone new and you said you weren't going to kiss on the first date and you definitely weren't going to sleep with him. Then before you know it, he convinced you to kiss him and kiss him and kiss him and... then your clothes start coming off. You know it's wrong, but he thinks it's no big deal. He told you just like the serpent told Eve, *"Ye shall not surely die."* As young people say these days, "What had happened was..." he pulled you right across your boundary line and into his pig pen.

Girl, you should know by now that touching leads to kissing and kissing will eventually lead to sexual acts. Play with fire and you'll get burned every time. Yes, that stove is hot. Stop touching it! He fooled you into believing what he had to offer was better than what God planned for you.

God would not choose a mate for you that would keep you from achieving your goals. He doesn't want anyone to cause you to forfeit your destiny and the purpose He has strategically planned for your life. I'm sure if you search your heart deeply you would find that there is something (dream, vision, goal) you've always wanted to do; possibly since your childhood. It's something that has been tugging at you for years. Something you thought you could shake. Even that man you dated thought he could shake it from your mind, but it still keeps coming up in your spirit. It's not going away because God put it in you a long time ago. It's a part of your purpose for being. Don't let anyone ever snatch that away from you and don't you run from it either.

As Mufasa said to Simba in Lion King, *"you are more than what you have become."* I encourage you to dust off your dreams and pursue after them with passion. There is something great you are destined to accomplish in your life and believe me, you have what it takes to make it happen. Press forward and don't look back because your future looks far greater than your past.

Pearls of Wisdom

- You are here on purpose.
- Don't let anyone talk you out of your dreams.
- If God placed it (vision, goal or dream) in your heart to do it, it's not going to lift from your heart until you do.
- Philippians 1:6!

The Velvet Lined Box #2
Displaced Pearls

Chapter 4: Giving Pearls Away

Giving something away means that you are giving something that is a part of you. If it's something that is of *value to you*, it will usually be given to someone who you really feel connected with. You give it to that person because *you believe that they will treat it and handle it properly*. The example of a mother giving her daughter pearls fits this description. If it's something that is *no longer valued in your eyes*, then it won't be difficult to give it away to anyone who wants it. The example of having costume jewelry and giving it away fits this description. Costume jewelry is something we usually find easier to give away then pearls. Only you can determine whether you are a pearl and whether you should be giving your pearls away.

Women are infamous for giving away things that are valuable; however, your heart and your body are two priceless parts of you that shouldn't be as easily accessible to anyone without them proving themselves first. Trust, commitment and love are some of the prerequisites for giving your heart and body to another individual. Usually this type of connection is found in a marriage.

For some of us, marriage is the only kind of relationship where we will unleash every part of us. Some women value themselves so much they've considered themselves worth the wait. They won't indulge in casual sex and they're definitely not giving away their hearts to the first person who petitions for it. They guard it with diligence as if they were a guard standing at a door making sure no unauthorized visitors come in.

On the other hand, if you're one of those women who are accustomed to giving your heart and body at a mere request for them, then I tend to believe that you have lost value for yourself. Losing value for yourself only causes you to possibly become a recipient of inappropriate treatment in your relationships. If you give it up, he'll take it and having respect for you will be out the door. You're no longer considered a pearl; you've diminished yourself to costume jewelry. Don't get offended. I'm not trying to put you down. You can do what you want. I just want you to consider your actions because they always have consequences.

People will treat you with respect once they recognize that you have respect for yourself. The minute they notice that you are willing to compromise your high standards of how you want to be treated, subtle acts of disrespect will appear. As the old cliché says, "give an inch and they'll take a yard." Swinish men are looking for that inch. At that point, they know it's only a matter of time before they'll take the yard.

Once again, your heart and your body are very precious and shouldn't be given away to just anybody. Everyone is not going to handle your heart properly. In Proverbs 4:23, it tells us we must keep and guard our hearts because the issues of life will flow out of it. When you freely give your heart out to a man (especially a "swinish" man) and he is not your fiancé (with a ring and a wedding date set), then you are susceptible to experiencing the trampling of your heart. Women tend to give their heart and body to a man simply because they believe they are in love. They also believe he loves them. Some men may really be in love, but a swinish man takes what you've given him and begins to treat it improperly because, in his mind, love has nothing to do with it. His intentions are to get as much sex from you as he can with no intentions of loving you right or marrying you. Take my advice, save the goodies for your husband!

A woman really shouldn't share her body intimately with anyone other than her husband. Your body is too precious and should not be given away to anyone that you casually meet. You definitely should not have sex the first time you meet a man. Some people call them one night stands, but the emotional tie usually far exceeds one night. When you give it up on the first request, normally the man will not respect you later.

When a woman gives it up so quickly, a man will then know that you are quick to have sex with anyone who asks. This will become the reputation that will precede you. He will become skeptical about you because he'll always be uncertain whether you may be quick to give it up to someone else when he's not in your presence. In his eyes, you are not the one he will consider for marriage. His goals with you will be short-term. He'll have you thinking things are well, but deep in his heart he knows that the relationship is only about getting the precious pearls between your legs and as much of it as he can. When he gets tired of that kind of relationship—and he will—he'll move on and marry someone else. Then your heart will be broken.

As we all know, a broken heart will mend with time, but giving your body to (having sex with) someone ties you to that person emotionally. Being intimate with someone makes you more vulnerable to them. It's almost like they have a slight bit of control over your emotions. Many women think that because he had sex with you it must mean that he loves you. He may even tell you that he loves you while he's having sex with you. I hate to be the one to bust your bubble, but he is only telling you he loves you in the midst of your hot sex because he is caught up in the feeling of your insides. If he loves you, he will wait. You are worth the wait. There shouldn't be any pressure neither should you feel obligated to have sex with a man just because you've dated him "awhile."

Another cliché that refers to women who give it up easily is this: "Why buy the cow if the milk is free?" If you're not giving the milk away, take your sign down. Your actions and willingness to give "it" away is an indication to men that your milk is free, available at anytime and anywhere. This should not be the kind of reputation that you want spread around about you. Your reputation is what goes before you. Most of the time before your mouth opens; your reputation has already spoken loud and clear.

An example of this is shared in the Bible in Ruth 3:11 when Boaz mentions to Ruth that the whole city was aware that she was a virtuous woman. Her reputation spoke loudly to everyone in the city. It was her reputation that caught Boaz's attention. The way she carried herself around him gained his respect for her. Notice that Boaz didn't mess over her by having sex with her, but he respected her and took the necessary steps to make Ruth his wife.

What are people saying about you? What are you known for? Are you proud of your reputation? These are some questions that you need to think about. Let it be known that you are a woman who highly respects herself and is full of ambition, hard working, sold out for God, dependable, and full of integrity.

It takes years to build a good reputation, but many of us know it can be easily destroyed by one incident. Take pride in maintaining a good reputation because it will follow you throughout your life. Clutch your pearls, girl! You are too valuable to God to be classified as a woman who quickly gives her body and heart to anyone who requests them. Let it be known that you respect yourself and demand to be respected.

Pearls of Wisdom

- People will treat you with respect once they recognize that you have respect for yourself.
- You are worth the wait; so make him wait.
- Your reputation speaks loudly even before you open your mouth.

Chapter 5: Throwing Pearls

One of the most unattractive displays of conduct is to see a woman trying her best to throw herself at a man. She will use her looks, her body and her words to lure a man her way. She is the type of woman who is always in a man's face hoping to get him even if he's already taken. She will grin in his face and pour on the flattery. She'll wear less and will make every effort to sway her hips seductively as she walks before him. If she wants him badly enough, she'll do whatever it takes to get him.

A woman may act this way because the man she is trying to flirt with is not paying her much attention. So to get his attention, she thinks she has to throw herself at him. She'll follow him like white on rice not even giving him an opportunity to breathe. Little does she know; throwing herself at a man shows that she is desperate. It's alright to let a man know that you are interested, but when you begin to become obsessed with catching his attention, then you've moved into desperation. Please spare yourself the embarrassment. You don't have to throw yourself at him. The look of it is distasteful. Women have to realize that if a man is interested in you, he will approach you.

When a woman is always in a man's face when he doesn't really desire for her to be, it could possibly make him feel smothered. A woman has to realize that smothering a man will never catch him; at least not his heart. You will have him for a moment, but when you smother him and hound him like a dog in heat, you will cause him to turn the other way. Most men will tell you that the women who throw themselves at them are not the ones they marry.

Whether you realize it or not, your body sends a signal to a man letting him know what kind of woman you are. He can detect this from afar off. This detection gives him a clear understanding of what kind of woman you are and whether he's interested. He may never tell you he recognizes your desperation, but he knows. He can tell when a woman is ready to give it up. He can tell when a woman is throwing her pearls at him. Throwing your pearls at him doesn't mean he won't refuse them, but once they're taken they'll never really be treasured.

A man also knows when a woman has set high standards for herself; one who highly respects herself and demands it. Its all in how you carry yourself, how you dress and it's within your conversation. Don't fret if a man doesn't want to be around you because of the high respect you have for yourself. Be thankful for not having to waste your time with someone who just isn't worthy of your presence; much less your pearls.

A man, as well as another woman, can tell when you are having your "hot" days. Even your mother and grandmother recognized your hot days. They knew when you were beginning to smell yourself. They knew when you were becoming frisky. Men can tell this about women because it's in our eyes, in how we dress, in our body language and in our conversation. Everything about you says, "I am willing to give it up." Your actions show that you are thriving for the attention of a man because it pacifies an inward area unfulfilled. You'll jump from man to man because you dread being alone; seeking to quench a thirst that is never satisfied. You will soon find out; however, that this unfulfilled area can never be filled by the arms of a natural man.

The woman at the well (John 4) had this same addiction. She kept getting thirsty. She kept throwing her pearls to men hoping to experience satisfaction. She thought her inner thirst would cease after her fifth husband, but to her surprise the emptiness inside of her remained. However, one day at the well, things changed for her. It was the day Jesus came to drink of the well.

That day He offered her to drink of the water that would cause her to never thirst again. She rejoiced because on that day her thirst was finally quenched. True satisfaction comes through your connection and relationship with God. He has the ability to quench any inward thirst you may have. Drink of His water so you'll never thirst again.

There is no need to throw yourself at any man because in the long run he won't respect you for it. Have more respect for yourself and let it be known in the city that you are a virtuous woman (Ruth 3). Whoever God has for you is for you.

Pearls of Wisdom

- Don't smother a man. Men don't like it when a woman is in their face too much. It is a complete turnoff.
- Put your sign up, "no more free milk."
- Your reputation will precede you. Make sure its saying the right things.
- True satisfaction comes through your relationship with God.

Chapter 6: Single Women and Married Men

Are you messing around with a married man? Has a married man been flirting with you? The Bible says that a man who commits adultery is void of understanding (Proverbs 5). In other words, he is a fool! But what is even more foolish is the woman who belittles herself to become entangled with a married man. This woman is foolish because, for one thing, there is no destiny in that kind of relationship. Someone always gets hurt and usually it is either the wife or the mistress. Nine times out of ten the husband is not going to leave his wife, especially if there are children involved. I know you want to believe he's going to leave his wife, but don't be a fool all day. It's not going to happen.

The question I have for you is: Why would you want to settle for that type of relationship? You are only selling yourself short of experiencing real love. He doesn't really need your consoling as much as he says he does. This is just an excuse to get the attention he desires. What he needs to do is rest his head in his own wife's bosom; not yours. He may even tell you that you are better than his wife and how you understand him and appreciate him more than his wife (blah, blah, blah...). He will make every effort to pour it on thick, but, sister, you are only seeing the sugar-coated version of this man. His wife sees the real deal. She knows him well. Much more than you think you do. Whether you know it or not, he may be escaping the ownership of his responsibilities and obligations to his household. In other words, he's not "manning" up. For all you know he may have cheated on her several times before he started cheating on her with you. He may be abusive and beats her daily. You don't really know. You just hear the wrong that she does. You are only hearing one side of the story. She may really love her husband, but the two of them are just going through some rough times. Don't allow yourself to be used as an instrument to destroy a marriage because you may very well reap that when you get married one day.

    Yes, she may not be treating him right. There may be some truth to his story concerning this, but, as long as he is legally married, he's not yours! And that also goes for those men who say they are separated from their wives but are still getting involved with other women prior to their divorce. They are the kind of men whom I call trying to get their cake and eat it too. During a man's time of separation, he'll run the game of playing you and his wife just as long as you'll play along with him. Ironically, you may actually find yourself falling in love with this man, but think about it: What if he decides to go back home? Your heart is all entangled in his web, your feet are anchored in his slop and then he says, "I want my wife back." Technically you can't get mad or throw a hissy fit because you were the one who opened your heart to a married man.

You may even say you like getting involved with married men because there are no strings attached, but that's where you're wrong. Whether you realize it or not, he's stringing you along the whole time. You're playing him and he's playing you. It's like the blind leading the blind. You both will end up in the ditch eventually.

While he's got the ring on his finger and the legal documents continue to record him as having a marital status, leave him alone and let him be man enough to get his business straight. Regardless of whether either of you want to acknowledge it, their hearts are still connected, they are still married, and you can't pursue a relationship with a married man. It's not biblical, and it's not ethical. Leave him alone and wait for your own! And that's all I have to say about that…and the married women said, AMEN!

Pearls of Wisdom

- All I have to say is don't mess with married men; ever.
- Settling for a relationship with a married man won't allow you to experience genuine love and commitment.
- If he's cheating on her; he'll cheat on you.
- Have respect for yourself and be woman enough to put that married man in his place. Send him back to his wife.

Chapter 7: Make Him Love You?

Many women have tried it, but I don't know how successful the outcome was. Some women will forsake their own life's ambitions to focus on getting a man to love them. Love is an innate desire we all possess. We may not want to admit it, but we all want to be loved. Nevertheless, I can't imagine wanting to be in a relationship where you're literally trying to make someone love you.

It is an emotional strain when you are trying to make someone love you. It's that way because you will always be the one giving love and you'll rarely receive it back. When a woman wants to make a man love her, she will give her all to capture the heart of a man when giving his heart to her is the farthest thought from his mind. Some women will compromise their virginity, their integrity, their money, forfeit their dreams, have sex with them, cook for them, some even use root (witchcraft) on them just to get a man in their arms to call their own. Being on the receiving end of love doesn't require a bribe. Love should flow freely from heart to heart without any manipulative or deceptive tactics to get it started. Love just happens. And if it's not just happening for you, maybe it was not meant to be—at least not with him.

A woman who longs for a man's love is not anything new. This kind of behavior has taken place back in the Bible days. This scenario is found in the biblical story of Jacob and Leah. Jacob loved Rachel who was Leah's sister. Even though Jacob had eyes for Rachel, Laban, Rachel's father tricked Jacob and gave him Leah to marry first. Throughout their marriage, Jacob openly longed for Rachel. Imagine being married knowing your husband is in love with someone else. Whew! That's a hard pill to swallow. Ironically, Jacob ended up marrying Rachel also, but inwardly Leah continued to long for Jacob's love. Leah continued with her wifely duties and birthed his children (Genesis 29:32-35). The names Leah gave her sons ironically give the impression of the longing she had for Jacob's love. At the birth of the first son she said, "Now my husband will love me." The second son she said, "Because the Lord knew I was hated." The third son she said, "Now my husband will be joined to me." Even after Leah gave Jacob sons; nothing changed. It was a fact: Jacob still loved Rachel the most. However, after that third son, something must have happened within Leah's heart. She had another son and named him Judah. She said, "Now I shall praise the Lord." And the Bible says she left from bearing. Leah must have realized the importance of putting God first instead of man. At that point in her life she redirected her thoughts and emotions to give God praise. She had to turn back to the relationship that mattered most. Even though many women try to get men to love them, there is a relationship that requires minimal effort on our part to receive love unconditionally. The wonderful thing about having a relationship with God is that you don't have to make him love you; He already does.

Besides, if a man loves another woman, don't play that foolish game of trying to take him away from her. You will look foolish in the end. Some women get a thrill out of trying to find out if they've got what it takes to steal a man from another woman. This strange woman (as the Bible calls her) wants to see if she can bring this man to a piece of bread (Proverbs 6:26). She wants to see if she can have him eating out of her hand. She doesn't care how you feel, or how much you've invested in the relationship; she just wants your man. I've got to ask this: Who in her right mind wants a stolen man? Somewhere down the line somebody will steal him from you. You reap what you sow; it's a law that can not be broken. Stay out of other people's relationships and wait for your own love experience. Besides, for all you know, he could be an undercover swine.

Oftentimes, when a woman is trying to make a man love her, the man will go along with the program only to get what he wants from her. A man knows when a woman is desperate for love. Somehow desperation oozes out of our pores and is detected by men who prey on desperate women. These kinds of men don't feel anything for you. Their main purpose is to sap you dry. You're giving it out and they're taking it. As long as you got the 'for sale' sign up, men will buy. Don't allow yourself to resort to desperate measures so you can rest in the arms of a man. Girl, grab you a teddy bear (that's right, I said it) and hold it real tight. Don't worry—it's only temporary because, in due season, a good man will come into your life to love you the way Christ loved the church. And the saved women waiting-on-a-husband said, "Amen!"

If you get involved with someone and recognize he's not really into you, don't waste your time. Throughout the relationship you will continually experience feelings of rejection because his heart is not ready to commit. You're hoping to walk down the aisle someday, but he is wondering how long he can play this game with you before you start pressuring him to really commit. If you have to convince, force, persuade or be deceitful to get someone to love you, it will never work. You will live a continual cycle of frustration trying to make that person love you.

Staying in a relationship for long periods of time hoping he'll finally pop the question can be frustrating. He says he loves you and you know you love him, but he's not willing to make that ultimate commitment after five years of dating. Obviously he's not that into you. Or either he has no intentions of walking down the aisle with you. You may need to move on. It's probably better that you find out now than much later in the relationship. Some women can't wait for a man to pop the question so they belittle themselves and ask him first. Not! This is a wrong move. Now for the remaining years the two of you are together, you will always be concerned as to whether he really loves you or whether he will remain in the relationship. At some point and time, he will feel coerced and you would've blocked the flow of his pursuit for you. A man likes to pursue a woman. Aggression is good, but a woman must keep it in perspective when involved in a relationship. No one wants to feel trapped or smothered in a relationship. It doesn't give the other person an opportunity to grow, and they won't love you properly. They will always feel pressured to please you.

Some women are convinced they are not only going to make someone love them, but they are also going to get married. Some women will settle for men who have no job, no money, no car, no goals, living with his momma (or living with you occasionally), not saved (no religious beliefs) and he shows signs of swine characteristics. And you want to make him love you? Hurry up and call 9-1-1 immediately because you must have bumped your head. You've got to be unconscious, or you're suffering from memory loss. Don't even waste your time or your emotions on a man like that. He shouldn't even be allowed to entertain your company. Obviously, he hasn't reached the proper level of maturity as a man. So how in the world do you think he's going to take care of you; much less love you?

Next thing you'll know he'll start hitting you a few times here and there. Because he's frustrated with his own life, he'll take it out on you. Before you know it, you begin to question yourself as to why he can't seem to love you. It's probably because he doesn't love himself and his life is not in tact. You'll run around like a chicken with her head cut off trying your best to do everything right to keep him happy. In case you didn't know, you're a pearl. You are precious in the eyesight of God. By no means were you ever supposed to be mistreated. Don't sell yourself short by allowing a man with such low standards to have your heart. Don't pursue after him either. Clutch your pearls, girl and keep moving. There is someone better for you.

I received another revelation while reading through Matthew 13:45-46. This merchant man was on a search for goodly pearls and when he found one, it was considered a great price. It was so valuable in his eyes that he sold everything he had to buy it. I said, "Wow! That is serious." The revelation I received was this: there is someone who is looking just for you, and, when he finds you and it is God's will, he will love you so much (the way Christ loved the Church) and forsake all (father and mother) to cleave to you (marry you). In other words, in his eyes you will be all that and a bag of chips with dip! Wait patiently for that kind of relationship and I guarantee there will be no regrets. You won't have to make him do anything; he'll want to do it on his own. That's the kind of love every woman wants to experience. Loving and being loved.

Pearls of Wisdom

- Love is not forced. Love just happens.
- If you made him love you, you will have to continue 'making' him throughout the relationship. This is not sincere and it's not from the heart.

Chapter 8: Why Does She Stay?

Many of us who see a woman in an unhealthy or abusive relationship often wonder, why does she stay? From the outside looking in we can clearly see that she's being mistreated and/or abused. Although this may be true, many women who are in abusive relationships and are dealing with it on a continual basis soon find themselves becoming numb to the abuse. This does not erase the fact that it's painful for them to be entangled in this kind of relationship, but many of them have denied it or covered it up for so long that it has become the norm. Many of them have come to the fork in the road, not knowing what to do and have accepted that this is how life is going to be for them.

Before we judge a woman who has been or is being abused, you have to understand her reasoning for accepting this kind of treatment. Anyone can say what they would and would not do when they aren't dealing with the situation, but if you actually had to walk in the shoes of an abused woman, your talk may change (I said; may). Listed below are a few reasons why she stays:

She has no money. Most women stay in relationships with men because of the financial security.

When a woman is involved in an abusive relationship, the man's main goal is to have control of her life, which also includes her money. Most women, married or single, allow their mates to handle the money matters, which leaves them dependent upon a man to sustain them. Many women don't leave the abusive relationship because they just don't have any money to survive on their own; so they stay. The man convinces her with his words that she couldn't possibly make it without him.

She has no where to go. Many women remain in abusive relationships because they really don't have anywhere to go. Because of her relationship with this man, many of her friends and family have been disconnected from her life. She's isolated and has no where to go. Leaving is especially hard for her if she has children. Initially, not many women want to succumb to living in a shelter. If her situation becomes unbearable, a shelter may be her only option.

She feels she doesn't deserve to be treated right. A lot of women get involved in abusive relationships or remain in them because they think they don't deserve to be treated right. This reasoning has a lot to do with a woman's self-image. Some women have a poor self-image because negativity has been embedded in their minds so deeply that it has become a part of them, which causes them to be drawn to these types of relationships. At times, she may feel as though this is as good as its going to get.

Abuse is common to her. Abuse is what she saw growing up. Everyone wants to be loved. It's a part of our makeup. However, the interpretation of how love should be displayed is contingent upon how it was displayed before us. Many of us learn ways to love based on our previous relationship experiences and what we have been exposed to while being raised by our parents.

If our home environment was filled with violence and abuse, then we tend to accept those types of relationships when they surface into our lives. However, that cycle does not have to continue and the change can begin with you. You don't have to accept those types of relationships. You deserve better treatment. Just because you saw "momma" get beat doesn't mean you have to. You have to tell yourself, "I won't allow a man to hit me; not even one time." Because if you let him hit you one time; another time will present itself. You have to break the cycle by not allowing yourself to get involved in unhealthy relationships.

Some women aren't willing to start over. For some women starting over may be challenging. Because they have been dependent upon a man to do everything, it will require them to come out of fear and out of their comfort zone. The average person, at times, finds that hard to do – so it is even more difficult for an abused woman. Starting over may be difficult at first, but in the long run it could work for your benefit; especially if it means escaping an abusive relationship. There are many resources available for women who want to break free and start over. You may not see it now because you are consumed by the abuse in the relationship, but the resources are there (find out where your local women's shelter and domestic violence organizations).

She suffers from dependency. Dependency plays a key role in abusive relationships. It is the goal of the abuser to gain control and cause his girlfriend/wife to become dependent upon him for everything. Because he has control of the finances and makes all the decisions, she will begin to lean on him. He will convince her that he is her bread and butter and there is no way she can make it without him. Because he is so crafty at what he does, she will believe him and become dependent upon him. His level of control over her will increase.

She has convinced herself to stay. In her mind she has convinced herself that this man loves her despite his abuse. She has convinced herself that she can't do better and believes no one will love her. She has convinced herself that there is a possibility that things will get better in the relationship. She hopes for this daily.

She is afraid of him. Fear is the ultimate reason why women remain in abusive relationships. After a period of time if you stay too long in that kind of relationship, fear will hold you there captive. If someone threatened you over and over or hit you several times, you would be afraid too. Women need to know that being in fear in a relationship is not love at all. Its one thing to respect a man, but if you are afraid of him, it's not love. It's abuse.

If you are a woman that is suffering from abuse (verbally, emotionally, physically or sexually), it is my prayer that God gives you the courage to break free. If you know someone who is being abused, please pray for them and get them some help (legal authorities and counseling). No one deserves to be mistreated. It was never God's plan (Jeremiah 29:11).

Pearls of Wisdom

- Staying in an abusive relationship is not going to make things better.
- Starting over is challenging initially, but can be very rewarding in the long run.
- Being afraid of your companion has nothing to do with love.
- If you're being abused, don't continue to walk in denial. Convince yourself to leave.

The Velvet Lined Box #3
The Pearl Snatcher

Chapter 9: Leanness to Your Soul

"And he gave them their request, but sent leanness into their soul." ~ Psalm 106:15, KJV

Sometimes people want something so badly that they will go to great lengths to get it. Initially, they are not concerned about the final outcome. All they know is that they want it, and they want it right away. Whether we realize it or not, there are some things that aren't meant for us to have. The reason being is that we're possibly not prepared for it, or simply because it could be bring leanness to our soul. Regardless of the answer no, some people are persistent and will continue to pursue after something that may not be in their best interest to have. These are people who will not take no for an answer, and they ignore all warning signs that say, "DO NOT ENTER," "ENTER AT YOUR OWN RISK," and "DEAD END." This is also true when women get involved in a relationship. Many women recognize the red flags, but totally disregard them because they want to have a man in their life so bad. They don't consider what they will suffer because of having him in their lives. Many of us live in the moment and don't think about the long-term results of the relationships we entangle ourselves in.

There was a time in my life when I got involved with someone whom I really wanted to be with only to find out it was the worst mistake I could've made. I ignored the warning signs and figured the person would change, which would cause them to change in how they treated me. I later found out that wasn't the case at all. I found myself settling for being mistreated and accepting the unsatisfactory feelings that I got from the relationship. I thought this was the best kind of love that I could get. Now I realize how foolish I was.

This is one of the reasons why I am writing this to you because I don't want you to waste your life settling for any guy that comes into your life. I don't want you to waste another thought with wondering if he will change, wondering will the verbal abuse continue forever, will he always curse you out when he's mad, will he blame you for everything going wrong in his life, or will the beatings ever stop. The answer is no. You must realize that you're not the cause for his mistreatment. He has his own internal issues that he must take responsibility for. You don't have the capability or power to change him. He will blame you for everything, but in actuality he is the one that needs to look at the man in the mirror. Whether he wants to admit it or not, he needs some serious help, but you are not his therapist; so don't try to be.

I am reminded of a situation that a young lady shared with me. She called me early one morning frightened about a dream that she had about her fiancé. She dreamed he was attacking some of her family members and then he tried to come after her. When he reached for her, he turned into a vampire and started biting her neck. She was awakened immediately as he bit her on the neck in the dream because she could actually feel him biting her physically. This was a few months prior to her wedding date. She asked me what I thought it meant and I told her I believed God was trying to tell her that this person she was planning to marry was going to change on her and it could be violent. I suggested that she reconsider marrying him or put off the wedding. I remember her telling me that she wasn't going to put the wedding off, but was going to go through with it. Her mind was made up and there was nothing I could do to change it. She made a choice. Remember, God will always give us fair warning before we do something that will harm us. He warns us because he doesn't want something to come upon us unaware nor does he want us to get hurt. He cares enough about us to let us know what He really prefers, but it's up to us to take heed to the instructions.

A month after her wedding, that fiancé (her husband then) physically fought her, picked up her body and threw it down on the floor of their bedroom (wooden floors; no carpet). She was knocked unconscious. They initially parted their ways, but eventually reconciled. Why did she go back? I really couldn't tell you. This is something only she can answer. Why do any women go back? This too, is a question that only women who experience these traumatic scenarios can answer.

Three months after her wedding, she and her husband were coming home in a cab from a wedding that they were in together. He had been drinking. They got into an argument and when the cab driver pulled up to the house; he pushed her out of the cab. She fell onto the pavement, bumped her head and was slightly unconscious again. She recalls that the cab driver drove off with her husband, leaving her there in the middle of the street. Neither of them knew if she was dead or alive. As she lay there, some guys coming from a party were walking down the street. They admired how pretty she looked in her gown (she had the gown on because she was part of the bridal party). They began talking amongst themselves about raping her. At that moment, a car comes down the street; the guys take off running and the man in the car stops and calls the police. I told her that God was watching over her and sent that man down that street at the right time. She realized then that this type of relationship would never last; it would only continue to bring leanness to her soul.

On the flip side of the coin, all of this could have been avoided had she taken heed to the dream that the Lord shared with her prior to those incidents. I truly believe warning comes before destruction. Don't ignore the warning signs in your relationships. Denying them or ignoring them could cost you your happiness, your peace or your very life. Too many women go into denial when they are being treated poorly in relationships. It is a defense mechanism that surfaces in our mind as an illusion to make us believe that the mistreatment is not really happening or that it's really not that bad. We often hear people tell us, "It could be worse." Women often say this phrase to soothe their pain. This statement may be true, but did you ever think it could be better. Women who build up this defense wall become numb to the mistreatment and settle for it. Don't fall for this and don't settle for it either.

I share this only because you have to be mindful of whom you allow to be in your life. Every guy you meet is not always the one for you. Sometimes women overlook the negative characteristics of a man just because they dread being alone.

Being alone doesn't mean you have to settle for being mistreated. And being alone doesn't necessarily mean that you are lonely. For one thing, God is always with you and He knows how to surround you with the right people if you just ask Him to. When women use the excuse of not wanting to be alone anymore, they set themselves up to fall for the next smooth-talking man that comes their way. Beware because people often say, "what looks good on the outside may be messed up on the inside" or "what looks good to you may not be good for you."

People often say, "You can't judge a book by its cover." What appears to look good to the eyes may not be good for you at all. This was originally learned in the Garden of Eden when Eve thought the fruit was pleasant to the eyes, but it was never meant to be eaten. Eating the fruit caused Adam and Eve to be banished from the garden. Those things that appear to be pleasant to the eyes may not be pleasant for your heart. Sometimes women get caught up with the outward appearance of a man and what he has to offer more so than his overall character and how well he will treat them. Often appearance deceives many. You have to understand, swinish men work hard to look appealing to the eyes of women, but inwardly they are an atomic bomb that can explode at any given time. The swinish man will dress himself up, be on his best behavior, wine and dine you in the beginning to win you over. He does this in hopes to get intertwined in your emotions. Access to your emotions will eventually give him access to your heart and then your body. Don't allow a few dates of superb treatment to cause you to melt in his arms. I encourage you to be prayerful about whom you allow yourself to get serious with. Don't be so quick to marry, but wait on the Lord to give you clear direction concerning your future mate. There are plenty of good men with character and integrity who will treat you right. They may not be perfect. Nobody is, but good men know how to respect and treat a lady.

Keep in mind that a smooth-talking swinish man has learned the skill of interacting socially with a woman.

He knows what to say and do to cause you to become desperate for his company. Some men play on that emotion of desperation when they sense it oozing out of a woman's spirit. They recognize you are lonely and will attempt to get whatever they want from you. Again, I must say this isn't the tactic of every man you will meet. One day, Mr. Right will really come and he will love you right. In the meantime, I don't want you to be persuaded to get involved in a relationship that is destined to bring leanness to your soul.

When that smooth-talking slick man comes your way during the time of your season of feeling lonely or desperate, you then find yourself asking God for him or you ask if he is the one. Or some women don't even consult God; they just jump at the first man who even looks at them for any extended length of time. Then the signs follow that show you to keep moving, but you hesitate and figure that he will change or you can change him. Sister, believe me when I say this: You are setting yourself up for failure. You might even say, "He's good enough," or, "He's workable, and I'm probably not going to find anybody better." Settling for 'good enough' in a relationship will set you up for leanness; especially if that person shows initial signs of mistreatment. If you sense any indication that there isn't something right in how he talks to you, treats you, how he conducts himself as a man or how he treats your children, then it's time to step back before you go any further because that relationship could very well be destined for leanness to your soul.

Have you ever had a friend that hooked up with a guy who wasn't really her type, but she went along with him anyway despite warnings from you and others. As the relationship progressed she began to complain about how he mistreats her, how he spoke to her negatively or cursed at her from time to time, how he seemed to be very dominant and then eventually she mentioned the first beating experience. She was devastated, and so were you. You were more devastated because, first of all, he hurt your friend, and, second of all, she continued to stay with him. You questioned within yourself, "Why would she stay?" Or, maybe you are the one in that type of relationship and you have questioned yourself, "Why am I staying?" "How did she or I get here?"

It all begins with how you value yourself. As you can recall before she met this guy she was beautiful, educated, a hard worker, and a good Christian woman and then the wrong connection was made. She hooked up with a swine-mentality man. Initially he was kind to her.

He made sure he dotted every "I" and crossed every "T;" especially when he was around people that she held in high esteem. He wanted to leave a lasting impression with them so that when he started acting indifferent; others would think she was fabricating the story or telling a flat-out lie.

After being with him a certain amount of time, you (her friend) noticed that she didn't take pride in her appearance (combing her hair, wearing clothing that made her look like a bum or too tight clothing) as she usually did. You (her friend) noticed that she stop coming to church regularly like she used to. Every time you called her on it she would make an excuse and would even tell you that he wanted her to do something else with him instead of going to church. You (her friend) even noticed that she began to isolate herself from you and whenever you would criticize him in any way she would defend him so aggressively that you thought she would fight you. What's happening with your friend is that her relationship with him has brought leanness to her soul.

Your connections with other people should not bring you down, but your life should be enhanced partly because of those connections. This also applies to the relationship you are having or will have. Your relationship with a man should bring enjoyment to your life and not create stress or fear. Be mindful of the warning signs and take heed to them because they will help you avoid unnecessary drama. Just keep in mind that the relationship that you decide to involve yourself in should never bring leanness to your soul (mentally, spiritually, physically, emotionally or financially).

Pearls of Wisdom

- If the relationship you're in constantly brings frustration, you need to consider whether the relationship is worth continuing.
- If you've lost more than you've gained in the relationship, you may need to move on.
- When you recognize the red flags in your relationship, don't ignore them. Taking heed to the warning signs will keep you from bringing leanness to your soul.

Chapter 10: Outshining Him

When you are involved in a relationship with a man who is insecure about himself or is overly jealous in nature you will soon find out that he doesn't ever want you to outshine him. He can't stand it when others think you are better than he is. In his mind he is superior, and anyone who makes him feel or look less than that has now become a target for trampling and rending. Swinish men ultimately don't want you to be blessed, to be encouraged, to prosper, or to be happy for that matter. They don't want you to fully exercise your talents, gifts or your abilities. They never want you to tap into the potential that you possess in fear of you outshining their own personal efforts.

If you have a plan for your life and goals you want to accomplish, these types of men will try their best to hinder it, block it or sabotage it. As long as you stay beneath them and dependent on them, they are comfortable with that. If you exceed them in any area; you are later belittled or what some call being "put in your place." Keep in mind that swinish men thrive on outward appearances. They love to be patted on the back and their egos stroked excessively. When that is diminished in any way by someone giving you that kind of attention, into the pig pen you go.

When he sees others praising your accomplishments instead of his, he will immediately become jealous of you. He will become envious of others acknowledging your efforts more than his. When you are in front of people he will go along with the praise, but as soon as the two of you are alone he will attack you with his words or maybe even his fist.

This is the same type of spirit that was upon Saul when he began to despise David. It all began when the women sang praises about how David had killed tens of thousands and Saul had only killed thousands (I Samuel 18:6-7). Saul was so jealous of David because he realized the Spirit of God was with David and he saw how others recognized the anointing on David's life. This is the problem of the "swinish" man. He knows that you are blessed. He knows that you are gifted, anointed and fearfully and wonderfully made and he can't stand it. He becomes jealous that you have everything together in your life and he's still struggling with his. When he sees you, he recognizes his own shortcomings. He doesn't want to face his shortcomings or deal with them, so he taunts you to attempt to bring you down to his level. He'll put you down and ridicule your success to make him look good. Recognize that how he acts or how he mistreats you is really not your fault. It's his own feelings of insecurity that cause him to act the way he does. Making you look bad to make himself look good creates an illusion in his mind that he's got everything together; however, slop is still all around him.

In efforts to make himself look good, he will become competitive with you. In his mind, he competes to become better than you. He will pursue his goals and possibly succeed, but the minute you accomplish something great, the criticism will follow. He'll tolerate your accomplishments, but he will not willingly celebrate them. The only time he will celebrate your accomplishments is when the two of you are in public because he wants others to think he's got your back. Little do people know that behind the scenes he is criticizing everything you do; making you feel as though you can't do anything right.

Of course everyone wants to share their accomplishments with someone. We share with the anticipation that others will join us in the celebration. Let's face it; everybody is not going to be excited about your accomplishments. If you are involved with a swinish man, you can forget receiving a pat on the back. As you progress in a relationship with a swinish man, you will find yourself becoming discouraged and hesitant about sharing your dreams and accomplishments with him because he will always find a way to degrade it. If you're not careful, he'll have you keeping your accomplishments on a hush-hush basis so you won't have to deal with the drama that follows because of your successes. Even though what you accomplished was really a big deal, he'll make you feel as though it was nothing.

You don't need anyone in your life who will not celebrate what you do. Every woman needs somebody in her corner. You want someone in your life that will encourage you throughout the entire process of utilizing your talents. A good man is never intimidated by your accomplishments, but is excited to be connected with a woman with vision. Even at times when you may feel like giving up, a good man will inspire you and encourage you to go after what God has placed in your spirit to do.

In a healthy, loving relationship both people endeavor to help each other make it. Neither one is concerned about who will outshine the other. Their main goal is to work together as a team ("together everyone accomplishes more") so that everyone involved achieves their goals. In the corporate world, the word used for others to combine their efforts to bring about something greater is "synergy." You want someone in your life who will work with you; not against you.

Don't allow someone in your life who tries to make you feel ashamed for what you have accomplished or for the talent, gifts or dreams you possess. Your abilities were placed in you for a divine purpose. Not utilizing those abilities, or allowing someone to belittle what you've been blessed with to make them look good, is ridiculous. If the man in your life is having a fit because of what you've accomplished now, he'll probably have a heart attack after God gets through working out what He really wants to take place in your life. My suggestion to you is to break away from any man that doesn't want to see you succeed in life. Connect with someone that believes in you and doesn't mind seeing you make it!

Pearls of Wisdom

- Allow people in your life who will celebrate you; not just tolerate you.

- Some men never want you to outshine them. They thrive on outward appearances. Don't hide your gift, talents and abilities just to please a man.
- A good man is never intimidated by your accomplishments. A good man will applaud a woman with vision.

Chapter 11: His Words

Words are powerful. They affect our thoughts, actions and our future. Words have the ability to make you cry, become filled with fear, become angry or even cause you to laugh hysterically. Words touch our lives in a variety of ways. Many of us can remember the childhood saying, "sticks and stones may break my bones, but names will never hurt me." At the time, we said it only to intimidate our opponent. Although we didn't want to show it at the time, some of those names hurt our feelings then and some of those words have continued to affect our adulthood. Any way you look at it, words affect us in many ways. In Proverb 18:21 it says, "Death and life are in the power of the tongue and they that love it shall eat the fruit thereof." The words we express over our lives have an impact on us and so do the words expressed to us by others.

We tend to allow the words of people we love or hold in high esteem to affect us the most. Their words carry weight in our lives. When you are in a relationship with someone you love, you tend to value their words simply because of your connection. Their words should not be critical, but they should be words that will encourage our lives. Of course there will be times when they will share constructive criticism with you for the purpose of helping you to see things differently. Diminishing your self-esteem is never their goal. Their words are meant to bring out the best in you.

There are some men who recognize the good in you and they feel threatened by your presence; so they will use negative words to destroy your self-esteem. After hearing the negative words so much, if you're not careful, you'll begin to believe them. If he can ever move you by his words, then you've entered onto his stage and as time progresses he will play you like a puppet. His words will have you second guessing about things you know to do. Your thoughts will become confusing to you because his words have begun to overpower your own thinking.

Swinish men use words to hurt, damage, discourage, to belittle and to inflict fear. They use derogatory words to immobilize you. No lady should be hit on, spoken to negatively, called derogatory (critical, belittling) names or mistreated in anyway. Never were you meant to be called a female dog (you know exactly what I'm saying). It is belittling and insulting. Their motive for using these words is to inflict fear into your heart so that you won't move forward in life. They select their words wisely with the intent to put you in an invisible box with hopes of you being afraid to get out. He'll have you so dependent upon him that you won't even know how to get out. Nine times out of ten, he's really a coward; an oversized bully, but because he roars at you like a lion you become afraid of him.

The swinish man snares you with his words so that you feel trapped. They repeat these derogatory words to you frequently so you will begin to believe their threats. In I Samuel 17 it describes the battle between David and Goliath. We are told that Goliath's words caused Saul and the people of Israel to be dismayed and greatly afraid. Goliath humiliated King Saul and Israel. Swinish men act similar to Goliath in that, they will try to humiliate you in public. The purpose is to display to others that you are incompetent and they are superior. If you hold a high position and are very influential, they will make every attempt to strip you of your influence and damage any impact you may have on other people's lives. This kind of behavior is also found in churches where the attendees are being spiritually abused by their leaders.

The Bible goes on to say in I Samuel 17:6 that Goliath came out and threatened the children of Israel for forty days consecutively that he would destroy them. Could you imagine a ten foot giant coming at you with the same threatening words for forty days straight? After awhile you'd be shaking in your boots too. Shaking is often how some women end up becoming as a result of some of the negative, derogatory words they hear from the swinish men in their lives on a continual basis. Shaking and believing. Be careful; this is right where some men want their women to be. He'll have you shaking because of his words that you'll barely know how to function. He wants you believing his threats so you would never consider challenging him.

If you start believing what he says about you, then you have symbolically crawled into a box. Only his words have the ability to get you out or to cause you to squirm while you're in the box. You have given this person too much power. They have put you in a prison, without bars; yet you act as if you can't get out or that you have no keys. You sit there and take it as if you are numb. Many women become so immune to the swine talk (verbal abuse) they no longer react. They start to believe saying anything or doing anything is useless.

The remarkable thing about David is he did something no one else did while being constantly confronted by Goliath for those forty days. David spoke words back to Goliath. David knew who he was and more so, he knew who his God was. Just because someone says something against you doesn't mean you have to believe it or accept it. David didn't accept what was being said by this giant. He spoke back.

You need to say something. Sometimes we are afraid to say something back because we fear the repercussions that come after. I know if you're in an abusive relationship, you're probably saying, "If I talk back, I'll get slapped back." Proceed with caution, but don't accept the abuse. If you can't say it to him, tell yourself to break free. Talk yourself right out of that unhealthy relationship. If you got talked into it, you can talk yourself out of it. You can always get the help you need if you want out of the relationship bad enough. There are plenty of domestic violence centers, programs and organizations that have been trained to get you out of an unhealthy relationship. You have to determine how bad you want to be free from that relationship.

Regardless of the negative words that have been spoken in your ears, you can make it. You can make it and you will make it. No matter what kind of unhealthy relationship you've gotten yourself entangled in, you deserve to be treated better. Don't allow someone's words to strip you powerless. Combat their words by speaking positively over your life. Surround yourself with positive people who will speak positive words into your life.

Here are a few words to ponder on: You are better off without him. You are better than what he gives you credit for. You can do anything you put your mind and hands to. He is not your bread and butter. Even though he has more money than you do now, doesn't mean it will be that way always. You really can make it without him. It may appear to be challenging to break free from the stronghold he has over you, but you will make it through. Others have lived to tell about it and so will you.

Pearls of Wisdom

- Words are powerful, but don't allow a man's negative words strip you powerless.
- Talk to yourself (yes, I said it). Tell yourself daily that you can make it.
- Talk yourself out of that unhealthy relationship.

Chapter 12: Pearls in Isolation

When you are involved with a swinish man, one of the first things he will do is isolate you from those you love. He wants to keep you close to him not because he's that into you, but because he doesn't want anyone to interfere with the relationship. He feels this way because he is concerned about outsiders sharing their negative input about him and how he treats you. He knows very well that if people you love know about his unhealthy characteristics, they will warn you and encourage you to leave.

Even though he abuses you or mistreats you in some way, he doesn't want you to leave him because that will make him look bad. So he will consistently try to convince you that the people you love are against him or they're jealous of your new relationship and obviously don't want you to be happy. If you're having problems in the relationship already, he will shift the blame off of him and tell you that your friends or family are the reason you two are having some issues in your relationship. He may even suggest that you all move away from them so the two of you can build your relationship. Building the relationship is not really on his mind, he just wants to isolate you from outside influences. To him they pose a threat for him to continue his manipulative and controlling behavior.

Every opportunity afforded to him, he will belittle and down play everyone you have a connection with. Little by little, you will begin to wean yourself away from your friends, family and your life as you knew it. He will begin to twist your thoughts to turn you against the people that matter the most in your life. He doesn't want them around you because he wants to control your thoughts, emotions and everything about you. After he has filled your mind with lies, you will become so confused that you won't know the difference between the truth and a lie. Before you know it, you will begin to believe the lie or the illusion without even considering the truth. Isolation includes a lot of brainwashing. This is what abusive men do initially to begin the cycle of running your life.

The next thing that will happen is you won't go to family gatherings and you'll avoid invitations extended by your friends for some simple girl talk. He'll have you feeling guilty about wanting to be with family and friends instead of being with him. He'll even raise a big fuss and create an argument with you when you want to go out with them. He may even ask you to choose between him and your family or friends. Because he raises such a fuss, you will eventually become discouraged about going anywhere with anyone or you'll become afraid to mention it because you know what you will have to deal with. You don't bring them up in general conversation because you don't want to deal with the drama that will follow.

You'll stop dreaming and you won't pursue after any of your goals because he'll object to just about anything to you try to do. You will constantly walk on eggshells because he has instilled fear in your heart. You will almost feel like you're paralyzed or trapped in a cage. You'll begin to look at everybody strange because your head is filled with his lies. Everybody you are close to will begin to look at you strange also because they know something isn't right with the man you call, Mr. Right. Case you didn't know, you're in isolation.

To isolate means to set apart from others. It's similar to being under quarantine. You can't leave and no one else can come in. A swinish man ultimately wants control over your life and putting you into isolation is his method of doing that. You see, he knows he's swine. Part of him can't understand why a woman like you would be involved with him anyway. He knows you're a pearl, but he's detected that you don't know it. Before you realize it, he's found a way to charm you right into his pig's pen.

There are reasons why a swinish man will want to isolate you from friends and family. Being in isolation causes you to suffer in silence because you have no one to tell what's going on in the relationship. A silence wall has slowly gone up around you and you have no contact from the outside to tell what you are really dealing with. Isolation also causes women to be totally dependent upon the man.

You may say, "This can't be happening to me." Get your head out of the sand and look around you. Where are your friends? Where is your family? If you can't remember the last time you've contacted them, you may very well be in isolation. If you are afraid to talk to or visit someone because he may go off on you or hit you, you're not only in isolation, but you are being abused.

If this is the case, you should strongly consider getting out of the relationship before it's too late. Don't even give yourself time to reason in your mind that there is a possibility things could work out. Or that this can't be happening to you. Yes, it can happen and it may be happening to you now.

Go back to civilization as you remember it to be and get connected to your friends and family again. They will be one of your sources of help to get you out of the pig's pen, off the quarantine list and out of isolation. There are too many opportunities and love experiences for you to encounter. Don't allow someone to block you or isolate you from that. Simply said, it's time to come out of isolation and get your life back.

Pearls of Wisdom

- Separating you from the one's you love is an indication that a man could be pushing you towards isolation.
- A man who constantly criticizes everyone you know and love is making preparations to move you into isolation. Don't believe the lies.
- A good man is comfortable with you being with friends and family.

Chapter 13: Stolen Pearls

Swinish men take things that don't belong to them. They don't care about the feelings of the person they've stolen from and how it could affect them. All they're concerned about is getting what they want; even if they steal it. I had a swinish man steal from me one day. I share this story for the first time only because I don't want you to ever think that it's acceptable for a man to steal your pearls from you. No one should be allowed to take something that doesn't belong to them. Your pearls belong to you and no one has a right to steal them.

The day he stole from me, everything happened so fast. I had no idea this was on his mind—at least not this way. One minute we were laughing, talking and sipping on a few drinks. I went to the restroom, came back out, took a few more sips of my drink and moments later, without warning; I was lying on my back. My clothes were off and he was on top of me having sex without my consent. From the time I took the last sip of my drink until he was having sex with me is a complete blur. I still can't remember anything in between that time frame. I don't how long it took me to pass out, how long it took for him to get my clothes off or how long we actually had sex. All I know is that I never got a chance to say no.

Initially it was just a date. We were just going to spend time together, but unfortunately this date ended up in rape. At the time, I knew nothing about date rape. All I knew was he took it from me. He stole my pearls.

Growing up as a young girl I was very sheltered by my parents and naïve to a lot of things. The night he took it from me I didn't even know what was happening. For years I was trying to figure out how I passed out and how he was able to have sex with me without me knowing. As time progressed there was more and more talk about the subject of date rape and the drugs used to initiate it. It wasn't until a few years later, after the incident, that I realized I was considered a victim of date rape.

This incident took place in my life more than twenty-five years ago. I only share this experience now to help another. Every woman must realize that your body belongs to you and no one—absolutely no one—has the right to have sex with you unless you have given them consent. Saying, "No," really means no, and if a man can't understand the words, "No," "Stop," and, "I don't want to;" then you're dealing with a man that has no respect for you. Sex was originally and still should be reserved for the wedding night. Waiting until the wedding night might sound old-fashioned, but it will save you from a whole lot of unnecessary emotional drama that follows after having sex when you're not married.

When I finally became conscious of what was happening, I can remember as he remained on top of me, how he continued to apologize to me. He continued to share how he wanted to show me how much he loved me. Love...? What a way to show it, I thought later. Many times I thought about this situation and I wondered why he took it from me. If he so-called loved me (I'm sure it was a strong like), why didn't he give me a chance to agree or disagree. I wasn't even given a choice. This definitely wasn't what love looked like, felt like or sounded like. Love is never deceptive. It is too pure. Don't allow someone who has an ill interpretation of love try to pass it on you. What they're feeling is not love; that urge is only lust. He doesn't deserve your love, or anything about you, if he uses deceptive tactics to get it.

Even though this young man was raised in a respectful home; he still had swinish characteristics. I later found out that he slipped something in my drink to cause me to pass out. I was so out of it even after he dropped me off to my parents' home that I don't even remember making it up the stairs that night. It is still a mystery until this day how I ended up in my bedroom. When he finally took me home, I can recall standing in the living room and watching my father walk upstairs after letting me into the house. From that point on....I don't remember. To this day, I've never asked my father what happened after he opened the door for me that night. I guess I've been too ashamed; thinking the whole incident was my fault. Looking back, I know now that it wasn't my fault at all. Recently, I realized I had nothing to be ashamed of.

If you've experienced date rape, rape or any type of sexual abuse, you have to realize it's not your fault either and you have nothing to be ashamed of. Thoughts of guilt and shame may try to fill your mind, but don't allow those thoughts to keep you from moving on with your life. The horrible act committed by this person is a result of their own emotional instability and deceptive ways. So it's nothing you did, nothing you said or what you wore *per se*; that act is just another example of what swinish men (men with unhealthy characteristics) will do.

As I was reading the Word of God, it was interesting to know that rape and sexual abuse also occurred in the Bible. In II Samuel 13, Amnon defiled Tamar. He deceived her by saying he was sick so she could take care of him. As she was feeding him, he used his strength to force her to lay with him. This is what these kinds of men do. They prey on your weakness for their advantage. In actuality if truth be told, they are the ones who are weak.

Also in Genesis 34, Jacob's only daughter, Dinah, was defiled by Shechem. He stole her pearls without consent and then he had a nerve to mention his love for her and requested her to be his wife (Genesis 34:4). However Jacob's sons weren't having it. They weren't going to allow Shechem to defile their sister and get away with it (read Genesis 34 in its entirety). Just like Shechem didn't get away with it, neither will the man who defiled you get away. Vengeance belongs to God and He will repay. Allow God to heal you, mend your heart and fight for you.

I tell you this story to bring awareness of the deceptive tactics that some men, with unhealthy characteristics, will use to get you. Some of them don't even know what it's like to be in love or to properly love someone else because they've never been taught how to love. It's sad to say, but a swinish man thinks attacking you is a part of love.

This selfish act of stealing my pearls was completely wrong and it had absolutely nothing to do with love. If you've experienced this yourself, please know it wasn't your fault. Don't beat yourself up with guilt. Don't allow yourself to walk around with feelings of being victimized because every person you meet doesn't want to sexually abuse you. Allow God to heal you and shower you with His love until you are strong enough. You are not alone and you will get through this.

Pearls of Wisdom

- Don't let your unfinished drink be unattended.
- You shouldn't feel pressured or obligated to have sex with a man.
- Don't allow a man to manipulate you into having sex with him. He may say, "If you love me, you'll do it." "I'll give you money if you have sex with me." Girl, don't be a fool because that's prostitution.

- Don't tease him with your body. Be firm when you say no to sex. No laughing or giggling. Don't give him the impression that you're willing to have sex when you're not.
- Call the police if you've been violated.

Chapter 14: Him and Your Children

One sign of how you can tell whether you are involved with a swinish man is how he treats your children. If your children feel uncomfortable around the person you are dating, you need to make a mental note of that and watch closely. Somehow children have this keen ability when it comes to judgment of character. It's got to be a gift because children usually recognize when someone is being sincere or not. Your children know whom they feel comfortable around and anything out of the ordinary will be easily detected by them. They will begin to act out towards you and possibly amongst their peers. They are possibly doing this not to get more attention, but they recognize something isn't right with the man you seem so desperately eager to cling to.

However, on the flip side of the coin, you must keep in mind that sometimes children will act unruly around your new friend because they are jealous of someone coming into their mother's life. They will fight for your attention, and this may cause some friction between you and your significant other. Watch closely with an unbiased objective so that you can clearly determine whether your child is acting out because they're jealous or because the person you are seeing is a candidate for the "swinish man" award.

If you notice that your male companion always finds a way to criticize or make fun of your child about their behavior, then you need to reconsider continuing a relationship with him. If he constantly puts your child down, it's like putting you down. Eventually he will put you down too. If he calls your child derogatory names, run because he's swine. If he touches your child inappropriately, call the police and never involve yourself with him again because he's swine to the tenth power.

Of course you cannot allow your children to dictate who you can and can not get involved with, but you should never allow someone to come between you and your children. You are all they have. You are their lifeline. To allow someone to severe that soul tie could alter their lives. Swine men like to be the center of attention, and they will try their best to create division between you and your children. Believe it or not, that grown man is actually jealous of the connection that you and your children have. He could be jealous either because he wants to be center stage in your life or he deeply desires that kind of connection and never experienced it in his life. So he divides it in your life because he never had it in his. This desire, if you may, could date back into his childhood or come from something he suffered in a previous relationship. In any case, being jealous of you and your children is not going to bring you and him closer.

If you're not in a serious relationship or in one that is not leading to marriage, then any man you date should not become familiar with your children, and your children should not become familiar with him. It will only cause more confusion in the eyes of your children when and if the relationship doesn't work out. Getting your children's hopes up high about possibly having a father in their lives will only create an unnecessary heartbreak. It's not good for your children to call everyone you date "uncle" knowing you really don't have that many brothers (or any, for that matter). It's best to keep your children as distant as possible from anyone you are dating until you know he is the one you are going to marry., Too many men around your children will show them that you can jump in and out of relationships at a drop of a hat. Remember, they are watching you to see how to handle relationships. Make sure you teach them well. Also, nowadays you have to be careful who you allow around your children because you don't know if the man you are dating is a child molester. Be careful.

The person you are dating shouldn't be allowed to discipline your children unless you are considering marriage. How the two of you discipline needs to be discussed prior to walking down the aisle. Make sure he disciplines and doesn't abuse. While you are dating, discipline is not his obligation. You shouldn't push your children off on someone else to raise them up. That responsibility belongs to you. If the relationship happens to not work out, they still have to listen to you. He shouldn't be more concerned about the well being of your children than you are. You are the mother and God is holding you accountable for nurturing them and training them in the right direction. Take more pride in motherhood. It's a ministry all by itself and it shouldn't be taken lightly. Neither should you allow any man to block you from answering the call of motherhood.

Don't allow the warmth of being in a man's arms keep you from your responsibility as a mother. Your top priority is to take care of you and your children. If he can't understand that you have to be there for your children, then maybe he is not worthy of your company. A swinish man could care less if you spend time with your children or not. He doesn't want your children to have more control over you or get more attention than him anyway. His actions will display his demand for you to choose between him and your children.

A good man would never want you to neglect your children. He recognizes the importance of mothering. Showing neglect to your children shows a man you will be negligent about other things in your life. It shows you as being selfish. When dating, initially he may feel slighted because he wants to spend as much time with you as possible. A good man; however, will be willing to compromise and work according to your schedule.

Sometimes men will try to provoke your children to anger to create division. They try to make your child angry, which will cause your child to react with disrespect. Then he will play on your emotions and tell you how disrespectful your child is. He will have you thoroughly convinced that your child is such a menace to society, and he will insist on reprimanding the child. In essence, what really happened is that your child has only reacted to his subtle provoking. You are your child's only defense, and if you don't stand for them they have no one. When your children see you defending him more than taking their side, they will feel hopeless. Make sure you listen to both sides of the story and then make a decision about what to do. If they no longer feel your support, they will then begin to resort to the world for the support and love they are lacking from you at home. Be careful, my sister. You know your child's overall behavior. If your child reacts indifferently, sit down and hear both sides.

The new man in your life should never physically put his hands on your children to hit them or fight them. He should never put his hands on your child for any reason—even if your child strikes first. He is the adult, and he should be man enough to walk away.

By no means am I saying that your child should dictate whom you date, but please be aware of how this man is treating and interacting with your children. If you decide to marry, you all must get along. If there are any red flags raised because of his treatment towards your children, they should strongly be evaluated before you continue any further in the relationship.

If you are a single parent, your first priority is mothering. You can't do everything your girlfriends without children are doing. They have no obligations to another person's life. Your presence and your love are far more needed than any money given. They need you.

Partying all night and coming home the next morning doesn't match with good mothering. Take time to talk with your children and listen to them. Make sure whomever you are dating is considerate of the well-being of you and your children.

Pearls of Wisdom

- You and your children are a package deal and if he can't handle the entire package, then he won't be able to handle your heart.
- Watch carefully of how your children act around the man you are dating. Sometimes they are able to detect swine characteristics before you will.
- No man should discipline your children unless marriage is in the near future (the ring on your finger and wedding date set).
- Don't allow a man to cause division between you and your children. You are all they have.
- Take pride in motherhood.

Chapter 15: Pray for Him

One night while I was in the process of writing this book, the Lord dropped something in my spirit, and I want to share it briefly in this chapter. The Lord simply said to put in a chapter about praying for the abuser, praying for the men who possess unhealthy characteristics that entangle women in their insecure webs. I know this seems farfetched because of what has been discussed in the previous chapters, but I'm just being obedient. We tend to focus on the victim simply because she has gone through the traumatic experience or because she has the physical bruises to prove she is being abused. Nevertheless, the abusive man needs just as much help, if not more as the woman being abused.

I'm sure no one actually wakes up one day and says, "I want to be an abuser." Whenever you ask a child what they want to be when they grow up, abuser is never one of the responses. This kind of behavior is something that is developed over time. It's a learned behavior that is passed down from generation to generation. Abusive behavior is something that is taught, seen, planted, and experienced by the abuser. Oftentimes, the reason they are abusing is because they've been abused themselves.

Because the issue hadn't been dealt with and his emotional scars have not healed, the cycle continues throughout his life. If he has children it will become a part of their lifestyles as well. Somebody has got to pray.

Just because he needs help doesn't mean you should remain in the relationship to try to help him. You're not his savior. Usually the woman who is suffering from the abuse can't help this man anyway. Counseling and much prayer are needed. I'm not saying you should stay in an abusive relationship and pray for him. Get out and pray! Put his name on the prayer list of every church you know if you want, but you shouldn't stay. When the Lord shared this with me I believe he meant to pray for these kinds of men as a whole. Not just one specific man or your man, but we must pray for all men who abuse so they can heal too.

Whether we know it or not, a man who is abusive is insecure and struggles with low self-esteem. He tries so hard to cover up his frailties by controlling and inflicting fear on his victim. This façade of being in control is only a means to expand his ego. It's all a show to make others think he's got it all together. He has to project this image to others—an image portraying that he has his woman and his household in check. If he didn't appear to others as being perfect, it would diminish the small amount of self-esteem he has. It's unfortunate, but he's been exposed to a false interpretation of love. He doesn't know how to give love or receive it. His mentality and thought processes are limited when it comes to having a healthy, loving relationship. He is closed-minded and believes his way is the only way. Anyone who comes against that belief better prepare herself for battle. This is why he is in need of prayer.

If truth doesn't get in and penetrate his heart, change will never occur. I encourage you to pray for abusive men all over the world. Pray for all the girlfriends, wives and children who suffer because of the abusive men in their lives. If you believe in the power of prayer, please take a moment to pray for all the people (men, women and children) who are struggling to break free from the yoke of abuse. This vicious cycle has got to end. Somebody has got to pray.

Pearls of Wisdom

- Praying for a man that is abusive and has unhealthy characteristics doesn't mean you need to remain in the relationship to do it.
- Abuse is a learned behavior and can be passed down to generations if therapeutic help is not provided.
- You can't save a man who does not want to be saved.

The Velvet Lined Box #4
Pearls in Waiting

Chapter 16: Pearls in Waiting

"Pearls in Waiting" are those women who are anticipating to become involved in a relationship that will eventually turn into a marriage. Waiting doesn't mean twiddling your thumbs, neither does it mean for you to sleep around with every guy you meet. While you wait you must guard your heart diligently and prepare yourself spiritually, physically, financially, and mentally for the man who will eventually be connected to your heart.

There are so many things to consider before getting involved in a relationship. Women must first think strongly about who they allow to have access to their heart. Realizing that any man that you allow to establish a relationship with you should never hurt you physically; he should never damage you emotionally, he shouldn't stunt your growth, or hinder your purpose for existence. If you're in a relationship like that, you need to know that you deserve better treatment than what you've been receiving. You have so much more to offer than what you've been given credit for.

This is why it's important for single women to be mindful of the kinds of men they connect with. Connecting to the right person and getting involved in a healthy relationship that will someday lead to marriage could have the ability to cause a woman to evolve in many areas of her life. Who you hook up with affects your future negatively or positively. Your future spouse should harmonize with your characteristics and your purpose. And you should harmonize with his.

The right time, the right place and the right kind of love is what God is strategically setting up just for you. As a woman, you already have the ability to make it, but with the right mate on your side it will create a positive influence, which will cause you to push positively throughout your life. Each person in the relationship has something rewarding to bring to it. By no means am I asserting that a woman must have a man, but I proclaim that whatever man finds her to be a good thing, she must be certain that he is worthy of her. If marriage is your destiny, then God will connect you with someone who will love, respect and cherish you. This is not something you can rush into, but this kind of love requires for you to wait patiently for it.

Unfortunately, sometimes during the waiting process, women tend to become impatient and settle for the first man who comes their way only to find out that they've connected themselves to swine. Little do they know that this kind of relationship has the potential of poisoning their lives. You might even hear some women say, "But a good man is hard to find," and they think they need to hop on the first train heading towards "Marriage Boulevard." First of all, you are not supposed to find anybody. The Bible clearly says that, "He that findeth a wife, findeth a good thing (Proverbs 18:22)."

All you need to do is allow God to work on you to help you become a good thing and leave the finding to the man. A man is not a fool. Remember, he was created in God's image, too. He knows what he likes and doesn't like in a woman and when he detects the right woman, the connection will be made. The connection is divine. Moving too fast and connecting with the wrong person could be detrimental to your mind, your health and your ability to love.

While you wait for this divine connection to take place, make sure you prepare yourself to be a wife. So many women are waiting for this good man to come into their lives to sweep them off their feet, pay their bills, be a father to their children and live happily ever after. They want the man to bring everything to the table, but when it comes time for some women to bring something to the table, they come short. Just as he is preparing himself to be a husband to you, you must prepare yourself to be a wife to him.

This will require for you to get your act together spiritually, financially, emotionally and physically. If your spirit isn't right and you don't have a close connection with God and your future spouse does, he'll detect it immediately. If you have a problem in your flesh where you don't apply self-control when it comes to sex, then how can you expect a man to respect you; much less marry you? If you sleep around the minute somebody just asks, a good man is not going to want to make you his wife because you can't be trusted. If you expect to be a millionaire and you can't balance a checkbook or budget five hundred dollars, what makes you think financial increase is going to come? You don't want to be the cause of your family not being able to pay bills on time. So get into practice now so that when the two of you get together you can build a nice nest egg of finances. If you're overly emotional and cry at a drop of a hat, how can your future spouse communicate with you? He will perceive that you're a weak woman who can't handle the least bit of pressure. You better learn how to lean on God in your weakness and draw from His strength because marriage requires for you to be strong during certain seasons of it.

Utilize this time of waiting to grow spiritually and to get some things in order in your own house. As the prophet Isaiah told Hezekiah, "set your house in order." Your future husband is not coming to fix you or fix your situation. That is too much pressure to place on a man. Keep in mind there could be a legitimate reason while you're still a pearl in waiting. Maybe you're just not ready. Allow God to work on you and to work on your future mate. When He's completed the work in both of you, you'll both be worth the wait.

Pearls of Wisdom

- Your season of singleness is preparation time for you to get some things in order in your life.
- Pearls in Waiting don't just twiddle their thumbs; they occupy themselves positively until he comes.
- Monitor the kinds of men you are connecting with. Ask yourself if these are the kinds of men you would consider marrying.

Chapter 17: Marriage

Getting married is a woman's desire that, for some of us, dates back into our childhood. Some women don't want to admit they want to be married, but the inward longing to be married is within them. For some, the idea of marriage has laid dormant because they're still waiting, but as soon as someone comes into their life, the desire to be married is revived. Keeping a proper perspective on marriage is important because marriage is a serious commitment. Pledging your love to someone for life shouldn't be taken lightly, and it shouldn't be jumped into quickly. Whenever you are hasty to marry you could find yourself hooking up with the wrong person. The man you thought was Mr. Right may not be right at all.

A woman shouldn't move so hastily to get married. A woman should consider dating a person for awhile so that she can get to know this person, his family and his overall character. You need to know how he will treat you. Learning that doesn't happen overnight. Take time to get to know him, and allow him to get to know you.

Getting to know each other doesn't necessarily mean living together. I personally don't agree with cohabitation before you say, "I do," but everyone has their own viewpoints on that, and we all will have to give an answer for our choices eventually. However, I don't think it's wise to play house, test-drive (sex) or shack (live together) to find out whether a person will love and respect you. If he loves you, he won't live off of you just to help him to survive. If he loves you, he won't try you out to see if he wants to commit his life to you. The concept of trying out each other doesn't make sense to me. What do you do if he test-drives you, you shack with him, help pay the bills and then one day you come home and he's taken all his things and left you a note saying, "This is not working out as I thought, and maybe we should go our separate ways and just be friends." So now you've given your heart, your love, your sex and shared the bills and he just kicked you to the curb. Swine to the tenth power! I'm sorry, either you love me or you don't. Either you want to commit or you don't. A man should be responsible enough to communicate the truth to you before he entangles your heart in his. This is why I suggest you to take time to get to know him and allow him to get to know you; with no masks. Be real with each other because, if you marry, all the things you tried to cover up while you were dating will come to the surface. Don't shock him like that; be real with him.

Another thing to consider before you run down the aisle is that whomever you marry will affect your life in many ways. Change will occur in your life after you say, "I do." Sometimes the change is good, and sometimes it is not. It just depends whom you hook up with.

Even though change is inevitable, some people say, "I'm not changing for anybody." "Whomever I marry will have to accept me for who I am." Yes, they will accept you for who you are initially, but eventually you will change and so will they. When you wear that ring, and take on his last name; change starts. Yes, change will happen in the relationship, but it won't happen overnight. Sometimes the change you are anticipating to happen in your mate may take years. It may take years for you to change as well, so you have to be patient with each other as you both grow and develop.

So many women are trying to rush a man down the aisle, plan an extravagant wedding, and spend thousands of dollars but forget about the day after the wedding. Women get caught up on their special day, which takes a year to plan but only lasts about five hours.

Many of us are guilty about planning the wedding, but we often neglect to plan for the life of the marriage.

Before you marry, goals, dreams, desires, responsibilities, and expectations should be clearly discussed and a plan should be put in place. Your future husband should have a vision and dreams he wants to accomplish for himself and for the two of you. Don't marry a man who has no vision. This kind of man doesn't know where he's going, and if you marry him you'll be going around in circles until he figures it out. A plan for the household should be in place also. Where will you two be in 1, 5 and 10 years? When are you going to have children and how many? Who will pay the bills? Will he be the sole provider in the home? Will you go to church? What church will you attend? Discussing your sexual desires and needs is important also.

The list goes on and on because marriage extends beyond the wedding day. When things aren't properly discussed then frustration and friction occur in the marriage. Communication is the key. If you don't talk about it, your mate will never know how you feel about it. Marriage is beyond the glitter and the glamour that takes place on the wedding day. Be very prayerful about whom you consider to marry because this is a choice that will have an effect on you beyond the day you say, "I do."

Pearls of Wisdom

- **Your financial status** – Does he have good credit? Is he broke? Is he a good steward over his finances? The answers to these questions will show you what you will be up against financially when you say I do. Lack of finances in the home can create stress in the relationship. Make sure you two discuss a financial plan for the marriage.

- **Your spiritual beliefs** – Is he a Christian? Does he practice a religion other than yours? You need to make sure your beliefs are the same because, if they're not, it could cause division in your home, especially when the children come.

- **Your means of sexual pleasure**– Sexual expectations should be discussed prior to marriage. What you will and will not do in bed needs to be discussed so there won't be any disappointments or frustrations. Be willing to satisfy and please each other (Hebrews 13:4a).

- **Your thinking** – His viewpoint will become yours on certain issues. Is he hasty in his decisions? Does he think things through? Does he have a balanced mind set? If he's double minded or indecisive, instability will fill your household (James 1:8).
- **Your associations** – Whom you marry has an influence on the people you connect or don't connect with. Take a moment to examine his friends. Are they positive people? Are they going after their goals? Do the men he associates with downplay their wives or cheat on them? Remember, these are the people he will take advice from.
- **Your children** – How will the two of you discipline your children? Who is ultimately responsible for raising the children? Children will change the relationship – so talk about how you will raise them.
- **Whether you will or will not achieve your goals and dreams** – The person you marry should be supportive of your dreams as well. If he isn't, then it could effect whether or not you will achieve them at all.

- **Your health** – If you're going to marry a swinish man, then your health will possibly be affected physically and mentally. If your husband is not health-conscious, you may not be either.
- **Your mental stability or instability** – If you marry a man with unhealthy characteristics, it will affect your mind set in a negative way. You will always be on edge. If you marry a good man, you will experience more peace of mind than the woman who marries a swinish man.

Chapter 18: Recognizing a Good Man

*"A REAL man, the kind of man a **woman** wants to give her life to, is one who will respect her dignity, who will honor her like the valuable treasure she is. A REAL man will not attempt to rip her precious **pearl** from its protective shell, or persuade her with charm to give away her treasure prematurely, but he will wait patiently until she willingly gives him the prize of her heart. A REAL man will cherish and care for that prize forever."*

~ Leslie Ludy, Christian Author & Speaker

Throughout this book I've shared various scenarios of relationships with men who have mistreated women, but as I've stated previously there a lot of good men in this world who are ready to meet a good woman just like you. Although, you may have encountered a toxic relationship previously, it's often hard to believe that you will ever get involved with a good man; much less recognize him when he comes. The next few lines will give you an idea of the characteristics of a good man.

I took a very informal survey over the internet to ask some women what characteristics they considered a good man should possess. The first response from all of them was that a good man should have a relationship with God. He recognizes that he is nothing without God and will submit to Him. A man who has a connection with God will be more prone to treating you properly. It is important the he not only hears the Word, but becomes a doer of the Word. A good man will make every effort to make the scriptures come alive in his life.

A good man is a praying man. A man who will cover you in prayer not only shows his sincerity in his walk with God, but it also shows that he is compassionate about your well being and the well being of his family. Covering you in prayer may not seem important to some women, but when you encounter a situation that only the hand of God can solve; you'll be thankful you had a praying man in your life.

A good man is a man of integrity. He doesn't compromise his reputation for a quick fix. He won't be sneaky or conniving. A man of integrity won't use deceptive tactics to access your heart. He finds strength in doing what is right.

A good man will build you up and encourage you to pursue your dreams. He is not the least bit jealous of your endeavors. No one wants a man in their life who tears them down or tries to secretly sabotage their dreams. A good man will do what he can to support what you believe in.

A good man won't force you to do anything you don't want to. He will not use any manipulative tactics to get what he wants from you. In his eyes, if you say, 'no' then you mean just that. He would never consider stealing your pearls.

Most men hardly ever want to admit when they're wrong, but a good man does not have a problem admitting when he is wrong. He won't have a problem owning up to his mistakes and taking responsibility for his actions. Because he cares about you, he will do what he can to make it right between the two of you—even if that means he has to change for the better.

A good man is secure in his manhood. He is not weak or timid, but recognizes his position to lead. Within his leadership capacity, he exercises that authority with confidence. He is a man of vision and direction. He is not wandering or trying to figure out what to do with his life. He has full assurance of the purpose for his life.

A good man won't mind spending his money on you. He won't look for you to reciprocate his efforts. He just wants to show you he knows how to take care of his woman. It's fine if you want to treat him from time to time, but don't fall into the trap of taking care of a man. It's not the right thing for a woman to do and it doesn't bring out the best in a man. Be careful not to take advantage of him if he starts to purchase things for you. If you're interested in him and possibly in love with him, some gifts can be accepted. Don't allow yourself to become a gold digger or to become manipulative in trying to get what you want just because he's being good to you. Remember, he has a heart too, and he doesn't like his to be broken either.

A good man will accept you and your children as a package deal. He recognizes your love for them and will respect that you need to spend time with them alone. A good man will be patient in gaining their love and trust. It may take time for all parties involved to adjust, but in time things will fall into place, if he's the one.

As a woman, make sure you have your ducks in a row also. Just as you expect him to have all these great qualities, make sure you are a woman worthy enough to have access to his heart as well. When you meet that good man, don't compromise your integrity. Don't throw your pearls at him, but let him know that you are a woman of value who is worthy of a good man.

Pearls of Wisdom

- A good man has a connection with God.
- A good man is a man of integrity and finds strength in doing what is right.
- A good man will recognize a good woman.

Speaking Engagements and Conferences

Stephanie L. McKenny is a licensed minister and an Associate Pastor at The Love Center Non-Denominational Church located in Sumter and Columbia, SC where her husband is the Sr. Pastor & Founder. She has facilitated various women's conferences (founder of Word for Women Ministries, Inc.) and is a dynamic preacher. She is available for speaking engagements, conferences and/or motivational speaking. She is the owner of J & J Publishing Company, which is a self-publishing company. The Clutch Your Pearls Newsletter is released quarterly. The theme of the newsletter is, ***"Loving You, Loving Relationships and Reaching Your Destiny."*** You can find more information on her website address is: www.stephaniemckenny.com.

If you would like to book Stephanie L. McKenny for a speaking engagement, you may do so by emailing her at: jjpublisher@yahoo.com and/or making a written request through mail to: P.O. Box 291205, Columbia, SC 29229.

PLEASE NOTE: After reading this book and you believe you or someone you know is being abused, please consult the nearest domestic violence agency for assistance. If it's an emergency, please call (911) for the nearest police headquarters for immediate assistance.

Made in the USA
Columbia, SC
20 February 2025